Searching the Future, Reviewing the Past

世界を語る、日本を語る

David Dykes

角岡賢一

photographs by
角岡賢一
©iStockphoto.com
The Yomiuri Shimbun
Jiji

Searching the Future, Reviewing the Past

Copyright © 2015 by David Dykes, Kenichi Kadooka

All rights reserved for Japan.
No part of this book may be reproduced in any form
without permission from Seibido Co., Ltd.

Preface

As the English title indicates, this book is about trends in the modern world. Most of the topics were first suggested by news events, but care was taken to research deeper and then to present everything from a particular angle of interest. For instance, in Chapter 1, the news behind the topic was the announcement of the Linear Shinkansen route between Shinagawa and Nagoya and the angle of interest was whether the planned delay of 18 years before the line can be extended to Osaka is realistic or not.

The Japanese title evokes another principle: that the book should be both about Japan and about the world. But this doesn't mean writing ten chapters on each. It is more a matter of recognizing that questions affecting Japan tend to be world questions as well and vice versa. Thus, UNESCO's inscription of *Washoku* as an intangible cultural heritage in 2013 coincided with a similar inscription of *Kimjang* (kimchi making) in Korea. In Chapter 17, the two examples are looked at together.

Other topic areas covered in this book include music promotion and distribution, food supply, sport, new technologies, energy policies, and activities for the preservation of local memories. The core of each chapter is an 800-word English text preceded by a vocabulary quiz and followed by a T / F comprehension exercise. More challenging practice is given with free-answer questions which could also serve as a lead into oral discussion, and a gap-fill summary text. For additional support, or else for light relief at the end, there is a rounding-off sidelight "column" in Japanese.

Thanks to Messrs. Kanno and Sato of Seibido for their patient guidance and support for this book. And above all, thanks – once again – to co-author Ken Kadooka.

Finally, although we did everything we could to keep chapter contents accurate and up to date, by the time the book comes out some facts will be sure to have changed. We trust that readers and teachers can counteract this with a little updating research of their own. But naturally, where there are other faults or inconsistencies remaining in the book, we will be most grateful to be told about them.

Enjoy reading.

David Dykes

はじめに

　本書は世界と日本で起こっているさまざまな話題を取り上げて、詳しい内容を英語で読みこなすように一冊にまとめました。各章では、硬軟の多様な話題を取り上げるように工夫しました。リニア新幹線や世界遺産など社会的なこと、ユーロ危機のような経済面、インターネット技術の進歩に伴う3次元印刷やソフトウエアの海賊版、臓器移植や「赤ちゃんゆりかご」というように医学と倫理にまたがる事象、オリンピックやニューヨークでのマラソン参加、女子選手という運動に関した話題など多方面から材料を集めました。分野が偏らないように、意図的に多方面から話題を集めるようにしました。自然・人文・社会科学というように、大学で選択した専門や学部に均等に各章の話題が散らばるようにも工夫したつもりです。

　日本の話題でも、読者の皆さんが知らないことが多いのではないでしょうか。リニア新幹線や富士山の世界遺産登録など、大まかに知っているつもりでも詳しく読んでみると新たな発見があることでしょう。そしてまた話題によっては、全く考えもしなかったような未知の世界もあるでしょう。各章の話題を通して、日本と世界への興味を広げてください。知的興味というのは、そのようにして広がったり深まったりするものです。特に語学教材としては、知的興味と語学力を関連づけなければなりません。話題に直結した単語を覚え、意味を読み取り、問題によって理解を深めていく――このような段階を踏んで、学習を進めてください。

　情報化が進んだ現代社会は、目まぐるしい速さで変化しています。インターネットの普及によって、瞬時に情報の検索ができるようになりました。これは「情報化社会」という側面においては、目覚ましい進展と言えるでしょう。しかし断片的な情報を集めるだけでは、社会そのものを深く理解することは不可能ではないでしょうか。例えば「この先、世の中がどのように変化していくか」を予想するには、深い洞察が必要です。インターネット上の検索で、簡単に答えが見つかるような問いだとは考えられません。このような問いに答える洞察力を養うためには、日頃から社会の動向に注意を向けるという努力が基礎になります。日本語だけではなく英語で高度な情報収集力が身に付いていれば、世界の出来事についての理解が深まることでしょう。

　最後に、本書を編集するに当たってお世話になった成美堂の菅野英一氏と佐藤公雄氏にこの場を借りてお礼を申し上げます。

著者記す

CONTENTS

Chapter 1: Shinagawa-Nagoya in 40 Minutes, 40 Meters beneath the Ground 1
　　　　　　＜品川ー名古屋間40分、地下40メートル＞

Chapter 2: AKB48 and the Music Promotion World 6
　　　　　　＜AKB48と売り出し戦略＞

Chapter 3: Mount Fuji: The Responsibilities of Heritage 11
　　　　　　＜責任が伴う世界文化遺産の富士山＞

Chapter 4: Tasty Vegetables: How much Extra would you Pay for them? 16
　　　　　　＜高級野菜、いくらまでなら払えますか＞

Chapter 5: Can Cars Drive themselves? And who is to Blame when they Crash? 21
　　　　　　＜車の自動運転、事故の責任は誰が…＞

Chapter 6: Germany's Departure from Nuclear Energy 26
　　　　　　＜ドイツの脱原発＞

Chapter 7: Lest the World Forget: History as Storytelling 31
　　　　　　＜世界が忘れないように──歴史の伝承＞

Chapter 8: Eel and Tuna: Tastes the Next Generation may never Know? 36
　　　　　　＜ウナギもマグロも、次世代では口に入らなくなるか＞

Chapter 9: Still Applying to Join the Euro 41
　　　　　　＜ユーロ圏、これからも拡大か＞

Chapter 10: Female Athletes Dramatized 46
　　　　　　＜脚光を浴びる女性運動選手＞

Chapter 11: Islands of Safety — or Baby Hatches? 51
　　　　　　＜安全の島という新生児施設＞

Chapter 12: Pirating and Streaming:
　　　　　　Paying our Share for Media Entertainment 56
　　　　　　＜違法ダウンロードに対応、音楽業界が有料配信へ＞

Chapter 13: Print-out Pistols: How Far should Freedoms Go? 61
　　　　　　＜3-Dプリンターで拳銃を製造：どこまでが許されるのか＞

Chapter 14: Smart Reality:
　　　　　　Computer Games Return to the Physical World 66
　　　　　　＜頭の良い現実──コンピューター・ゲームが現実世界に復帰＞

Chapter 15: Seven Days, Six Nights and a Run:
　　　　　　A Special Interest Tour 71
　　　　　　＜6泊7日でマラソン参加──特別企画ツアー＞

Chapter 16: Fracking: Cracks in the Ground beneath our Feet 76
　　　　　　＜水圧破砕法によるシェールガス・オイル採取で足下の地面にひび＞

Chapter 17: Two World Heritage Food Traditions:
　　　　　　Washoku and Kimchi 81
　　　　　　＜和食とキムチ、世界無形文化遺産に＞

Chapter 18: A Restored View of Old Edo? 86
　　　　　　＜江戸の景観を取り戻す＞

Chapter 19: Cross-border Organ Transplants 91
　　　　　　＜国境を越えた臓器移植＞

Chapter 20: The Next Two Summer Olympics: Rio and Tokyo 96
　　　　　　＜リオデジャネイロと東京の五輪＞

Shinagawa-Nagoya in 40 Minutes, 40 Meters beneath the Ground

CHAPTER 1

　JR東海が主体となって、時速500キロで品川と名古屋を40分で結ぶリニア中央新幹線が2027年開業を目指して始動しました。品川駅も名古屋駅も地下駅ですが、着工に向けて準備が進んでいるようです。用地買収が不要な大深度の地下40メートルを走る区間が多いため、全線の9割近くがトンネルです。大阪までの同時開業を望む声も多いのですが、工事費を一挙に負担することを避けるために大阪までの延伸は2045年の予定です。

リニア新幹線の試験車両

VOCABULARY

Match these expressions from the text with the items closest in meaning in the box below.

(1) landmark ___　(2) replacement ___　(3) rooftop ___　(4) hurtle ___
(5) precaution ___　(6) unviable ___　(7) bonanza ___　(8) nostalgic ___

a. substitute	b. not feasible	c. shoot very fast	d. fondly regretful
e. lucky bonus	f. conspicuous and well-known		
g. outside on the the uppermost floor		h. preventive measure	

1

READING

At the start of 2014, the zone north of Nagoya JR Station was an enormous construction site. Three **landmark**[1] buildings had been pulled down and foundations were being laid for their **replacements**.[2] These new structures are due to begin opening in 2015. Two of them will be linked by "sky streets" on their second and 15th floors to similar promenade decks already in place above the south side of the station, completing walkways, shopping floors and restaurant galleries that run for hundreds of meters. Across the traffic circle in front of the station, the third building will feature a **rooftop**[3] garden halfway up, offering views of this ensemble. But what excites local business people most is the part of the project that will never be visible in a sweep of the eye because it is deep underground. Intersecting at 90 degrees with the northern end of the Tokaido Shinkansen platforms, but 30 meters lower down, will be platforms for the Linear Shinkansen, or to use its official name, the Central Shinkansen.

As has been widely reported, this wheel-less and frictionless train is due to come into service in 2027 between Tokyo (Shinagawa) and Nagoya, covering the 286 km in 40 minutes, compared with 100 minutes for the fastest Nozomi services between Tokyo (Station) and Nagoya. For most people it will be an unfamiliar experience, **hurtling**[4] at a top speed of 500 kph along a route that stays 86 percent underground. On the way there will be a stretch where the train surfaces to offer the reverse view of Mount Fuji from the one seen on the Tokaido route. The likely ticket price will be about ¥700 higher than for the Nozomi.

The reason for relying on tunnels is partly to solve the engineering problem of crossing the Southern Alps. It also makes sense as an earthquake **precaution**,[5] since underground tremors are smaller. But there is an economic side to it as well. Since 2000, Japan has a law allowing free use of underground space for public projects. Essentially, a constructor building an important piece of infrastructure does not need to buy the land for it in places where it lies more than 40 meters underground. Without this, costs for the new line would explode making the project **unviable**.[6] Tickets would cost more than users would be willing to pay.

Cost balancing is vital to JR Tokai, the company planning the project. Of course, the prefectures and cities served by the line will also contribute to its

Chapter 1 Shinagawa-Nagoya in 40 Minutes, 40 Meters beneath the Ground

costs. But in the long run, the company wants the project to pay for itself out of passengers' fares. This was also the main reason, the company explained in September 2013, why the line had to end at Nagoya in 2027. To take it as far as Osaka at that stage would mean borrowing more money than the company feels able to repay. It will only be after quite a long recovery pause of 18 years that the linear train finally makes it to Kansai, in 2045. At least, that is the current thinking.

In Nagoya, this view of things seems wise enough. Beginning already with the batch of new buildings around the JR station, it seems that the city can look forward to a **bonanza**[7] of a 30-year advantage over its western rival, which will have only one high-speed rail link to Tokyo. Already, Nagoya and the surrounding region are looking for ways of providing smooth links from the future station to Chubu International Airport and other surrounding cities and transportation hubs. Government and business symposiums are being held on how to lift Nagoya into a role it has never quite had before in the eyes of outsiders — a "fun" city.

More darkly, there are also people who see this as a return for the "Nagoya Passing" insult of 1992, when the first generation of Nozomi trains ran between Tokyo and Osaka for a year stopping at Shin-Yokohama but passing Nagoya and Kyoto.

It was no great surprise in December 2013 when the assembled business and government world of Osaka staged a protest conference demanding "Ōsaka dōji kaigyō" — the simultaneous opening of the line as far as Osaka. The initial reaction from JR Tokai was simply another objection that this would result in unsustainable borrowing debts. However, the announcement of the route and station details for the western section followed remarkably soon, in January 2014, and if the pressure from Osaka continues, it may still turn out that the Nagoya Bonanza, like the Nagoya Passing, will be shorter-lived than originally expected.

Older people looking at these regional and financial tensions may feel **nostalgic**[8] for the first Shinkansen project, which moved from planning approval in 1958 to the opening of the Tokyo-Osaka line in time for the 1964 Olympics. Admittedly, things only moved so fast then because of political pushing, which hopefully now belongs to the past.

NOTES

promenade deck「歩行者用通路」 **ensemble**「複合建築」 **infrastructure**「(道路や鉄道などの)社会的基盤」 **symposium**「シンポジウム」数人のパネリストが特定の話題について討論する。複数形はsymposia, symposiums **Nagoya Passing**「名古屋通過」東海道新幹線で「のぞみ」新設当初、一部の列車で名古屋と京都に停車せず通過していたことを指す。 **the route and station details for the western section**「名古屋以西の経路と駅の詳細」

TRUE / FALSE

Mark these statements true (T) or false (F).

1. The Central Shinkansen platform at Nagoya will run parallel to the one for the Tokaido Shinkansen. [T / F]

2. Earthquake tremors are usually felt more strongly underground. [T / F]

3. The line is planned to end in Nagoya in 2027 for financial reasons. [T / F]

4. For several years, Nozomi trains did not stop at Nagoya or Kyoto. [T / F]

5. If the pressure from Osaka continues, there seems to be a good chance of the line being extended earlier than announced. [T / F]

6. Building the first Shinkansen line between Tokyo and Osaka took only six years. [T / F]

COMPREHENSION

Answer the questions in English.

1. "Sixty minutes will be cut off the traveling time between Tokyo and Nagoya." — Explain why this isn't quite true.

   _____

2. How would it affect the construction costs if JR Tokai were to build closer to the surface?

   _____

3. What great bonanza will the line bring to Nagoya up until 2045?

   _____

4. Who attended the meeting in Osaka in December 2013 to call for a planning change?

   _____

Chapter 1 Shinagawa-Nagoya in 40 Minutes, 40 Meters beneath the Ground

5. Why did the construction of the first Shinkansen line go ahead so fast?
   _____

GUIDED SUMMARY   CD1-5

Fill in the blanks with the words listed below.

In 2027, the linear motor trains on the Central Shinkansen Line will ($_1$_____) Shinagawa and Nagoya in 40 minutes. These trains will travel without ($_2$_____), shooting along on a magnetic field at a maximum operating speed of 500 kph. Nearly 90 percent of the route will run ($_3$_____), mainly in order to avoid land purchase expenses. Once the line reaches Nagoya, the city can expect to enjoy considerable business ($_4$_____) over Osaka. People in Osaka naturally want to have the ($_5$_____) built as early as possible, but the constructor, JR Tokai, insists that it is ($_6$_____) difficult to complete this project in one push. A recovery phase will be required first, in which to pay off the initial borrowing debts.

---
wheels   advantages   underground   financially   connect   extension
---

COLUMN

東海道新幹線の東京－新大阪間が開業したのはオリンピックが開かれた1964年、山陽新幹線として博多まで延伸されたのは11年後でした。開業当時の営業速度は時速210キロ、ひかりとこだまが1時間に1本ずつというのんびりした時代でした。世界で超高速鉄道の先駆けとなった日本の新幹線ですが、欧州ではフランスのTGV（Train à Grande Vitesse、1981年開業）やドイツのICE（Inter-city Express）も独自の技術を持っています。上海の浦東国際空港と市内を結ぶ区間で、リニアモーターカー路線が実用化されています。技術的に時速400キロを出すことが可能ですが、消費電力などの実用面から時速300キロで営業運転を行っています。

CHAPTER 2

AKB 48 and the Music Promotion World

　AKB48がデビューしたのは2006年でした。直後の数年は地元の秋葉原でファンと握手会をするほどのんびりした出発だったのですが、人気に火が付いてからはそれどころではなくなりました。国内外に、似たようなグループが続々と誕生しています。1980年代後半に一世を風靡（ふうび）したおニャン子クラブの教訓などを活かし、人気が持続するような工夫を次々に実行に移しています。"総選挙"などは、その1つです。

秋葉原にあるAKB48劇場

VOCABULARY

Match these expressions from the text with the items closest in meaning in the box below.

(1) fluctuate ___   (2) defy ___   (3) rotate ___   (4) modest ___
(5) cohort ___   (6) smash ___   (7) stroke of genius ___   (8) favoritism ___

a. hugely successful	b. keep changing	c. group of companions	d. only so-so
e. a brilliant idea	f. refuse to obey	g. perform in turn	
h. treating some people better than others			

Chapter 2 AKB 48 and the Music Promotion World

READING

The girl group AKB48 began performing in 2006 and attracted international interest in 2011 when they got into *Guinness World Records* as the world's largest pop group with 48 members. Actually, the exact number **fluctuates**.[1]

What is truly remarkable about AKB48, though, is their sales performance. As of February 2014, their last 21 singles had all topped the Japanese Oricon charts, and 17 of them had sold more than a million. In comparison, the Morning Musume group, who started in 1997, reached a million only three times. CD and DVD sales are supposed to be falling now due to technology change, but AKB48 is **defying**[2] the trend. Their 2013 hit *Sayonara Crawl* passed two million — a record for female artists in Japan.

The story of AKB48's early years can be found on their official website. Producer Yasushi Akimoto started in 2005 with the idea of a group close to the fans — artists you can talk to. As a base, he set up a live stage in the Don Quijote store in Akihabara and recruited three teams of 16 girls each to **rotate**[3] in daily shows. After performances, the artists would line up to shake hands with fans at the door. This "small theater" tradition still continues, although tickets are only available by lottery now.

Success was **modest**[4] at first. Sales only began climbing in 2008. But then in October 2009, *River* was the group's first single to reach number one in Oricon, and a year later *Beginner* was their first million-selling hit. Since then, all of their singles have gone to the top, and all except one have sold a million. There has been organization expansion, too, resulting in "sister groups" in Nagoya (SKE48), Osaka (NMB48), and Fukuoka (HKT48), and overseas in Jakarta and Shanghai. The groups are all similarly organized, and there are occasional joint concerts and exchanges of members.

After two or three years, most girls are "graduated" out. Some of these continue as more mature artists under Akimoto's direction, while others change agents or retire. Graduating members are replaced by "trainees" or through casting.

Many of these features are not original. Mass castings and trainees in reserve were typical of Johnny and Associates, which produced boy groups in the 1980s; and year-**cohorts**,[5] team leaders and graduations are familiar from the Hello! Project, which produced Morning Musume. Even the letters AKB recall NGK, the abbreviation for Namba Grand Kagetsu, the Osaka stage of the Yoshimoto

Creative Agency. The idea of a daily show given by three teams in rotation is an NGK tradition, and NMB48 has its stage in the NGK basement.

A point more unique to Yasushi Akimoto is the attention he pays to fan ratings of group members. This goes a long way back to his experience with the girl group Onyanko Club (1985), whose first members were selected by a studio audience vote on TV. The selected girls were given a TV series, and surprised everyone by turning out **smash**[6] hits. Less positively, the project began to attract complaints that it was corrupting school students. But at any rate, it demonstrated the potential of audience ratings as a means of matching entertainment to fans' preferences, for good or for bad. In some ways, AKB48 is a more cautious development of the Onyanko Club model.

Since 2009, fan preferences in AKB48 are obtained through "general elections." All members of AKB48 and its Japanese sister groups can be voted for, and the immediate point is to decide who takes "center position" in a forthcoming song. But the overall result is also used as a reference for deciding who has to leave the group, who will be moved to a different team, or who will play an important part in future events and promotions.

The **stroke of genius**[7] in the system is that the voting slip is contained in a particular CD or DVD, which fans have to buy if they wish to vote. Thus in addition to advertising the next song, the election also boosts the sales of the last one. That seems to be the reason why AKB48 singles go on breaking records while the rest of the music market is shrinking. It is an elegant plan, but one which only works on a sustained wave of popularity. It will be interesting to see how much further the wave can carry it.

Life for AKB48 members is not always happy. The pressure of having to compete to please fans is stressful, and there have been several media reports of emotional breakdowns. Akimoto recognizes this, but points out that producer **favoritism**[8] would be equally painful and less fair. To correct the pressure, he takes a few of his decisions on a "stone-paper-scissors" basis, which may bring a lucky break to some under-recognized group member. In addition, the same insistence on keeping performers "close to the fans" also leads to overexcitement on the part of some fans, as was seen in one person's attempt to slash group members with a saw at a handshaking event in May 2014.

Chapter 2 AKB 48 and the Music Promotion World

NOTES

the Oricon charts 「オリコン・チャート」音楽情報会社オリコン（英文社名はOricon Inc.）が提供する日本国内の音楽ヒットチャート **Yasushi Akimoto** 秋元康(1958-)放送作家・作詞家で、AKB48のプロデューサー **Johnny and Associates**「株式会社ジャニーズ事務所」 **Hello! Project**「ハロー！プロジェクト」芸能事務所アップフロントプロモーションに所属する女子アイドルグループなどの総称 **Morning Musume**「モーニング娘。」1998年にデビューした女子アイドルグループ **Namba Grand Kagetsu**「なんばグランド花月」吉本興業直営で、大阪市難波にある劇場 **Onyanko Club**「おニャン子クラブ」1985年のテレビ番組から生まれた女性アイドルグループ。プロデューサーは秋元康氏。1987年解散。

TRUE / FALSE

Mark these statements true (T) or false (F).

1. AKB48 became instantly popular when they began performing in 2006. [T / F]

2. The producer's idea of being "close to the fans" took the form of shaking hands at the door after each performance. [T / F]

3. The sales of singles began to rise modestly from late 2009 on. [T / F]

4. Most members remain in the group for five or six years. [T / F]

5. Getting AKB48 fans to give their favorite group members ratings was a rather original idea. [T / F]

6. In general elections, the immediate question voted on is who is to be put in "center position" for a new song. [T / F]

COMPREHENSION

Answer the questions in English.

1. What is the cause behind the recent fall in most CD and DVD sales?

2. What has Akimoto's organization expansion resulted in?

3. What started to go wrong with Akimoto's earlier girl group Onyanko Club?

4. What do fans have to do if they want to vote in a general election?

5. What seems to have been behind the emotional breakdowns of some AKB48 members?

___

GUIDED SUMMARY　　　　　　　　　　　　　　　　　CD1-9

Fill in the blanks with the words listed below.

AKB48 began to enjoy real (1_____) in 2008, and have achieved million (2_____) with nearly all of their songs since then. Their (3_____), Yasushi Akimoto, created a previous girl group called Onyanko Club in the 1980s, but his control of AKB48 is tighter. The (4_____) of genius in his system is the holding of "general elections" in which fans vote for who is to take center position in new songs. The (5_____) slips are contained in CDs and DVDs. Through this, Akimoto controls both the group members and their fans. The stress from all this control is quite strong, and there have been several emotional (6_____) in the group.

stroke	popularity	voting	breakdowns	producer	sales

COLUMN

　インターネットが普及し、CDやDVDの売り上げに影響を及ぼしています。ユーチューブやニコニコ動画のようにインターネット上では、無限と言って良いほど無料で動画を見ることができます。アイドルの世界も、百万枚単位でレコードが売れた時代からは様変わりでしょう。そんな中にあって、"投票権"を付けたCDなどを売る「総選挙」というのは、画期的な考えのようにも思えます。

　歌手などを、一人ではなくて集団で売り出すのは今に始まったことではありません。1960年代には「グループ・サウンズ」の時代がありました。ザ・タイガースやブルー・コメッツなど人気グループが続出しましたが、長くは続きませんでした。男性グループの売り出しを得意としているのがジャニーズ事務所ですね。

Mount Fuji: The Responsibilities of Heritage

CHAPTER 3

　2013年6月、富士山が世界遺産に登録されました。以前に自然遺産として登録しようとして断念した経緯がありました。ユネスコの世界遺産委員会は今回、文化遺産として日本政府が推薦した富士山（正式名称：富士山――信仰の対象と芸術の源泉）の登録をしました。浅間神社などと併せて文化遺産として申請したのが功を奏したようです。しかし山上のごみ処理問題など、解決すべき課題も多くみられます。世界遺産登録によって登山者数が増加することが見込まれ、適切な対応が求められています。

宝永噴火口が見える角度からの富士山

VOCABULARY

Match these expressions from the text with the items closest in meaning in the box below.

(1) approve ___　(2) improve ___　(3) icon ___　(4) strategy ___
(5) esthetic ___　(6) restore ___　(7) voluntary ___　(8) compulsory ___

| a. obligatory | b. symbol | c. accept | d. artistic | e. return to their earlier condition |
| f. non-obligatory | | g. make better | | h. plan of action |

11

When Mount Fuji was **approved**[1] for registration as a UNESCO world cultural heritage site in June 2013, one of the committee members who had voted for it said in an interview afterward that he was surprised it wasn't already registered.

As a matter of fact, there had been an attempt to have the mountain recommended in 2003, but as a natural heritage site. This was soon abandoned, however, because it looked likely to fail. The most widely reported reason for this was uncontrolled trash dumping and the primitive state of the trailside toilets. But things like that can be **improved**,[2] and soon were. A more fundamental reason was harder to deal with; Mount Fuji may be an **icon**[3] for Japan, but in world terms, a 3,776-meter conical volcano just isn't all that special.

There were also changes in outlook in the World Heritage Committee around that time, with less insistence on the difference between cultural and natural sites as well as a trend away from single objects such as mountains or castles to series of sites connected through a common activity. A good example was the heritage site in the Kii Peninsula mountains, registered in 2004. It included two religious routes, 14 shrines and temples and three areas of landscape.

The 2013 application for Mount Fuji followed a similar **strategy**.[4] Along with the mountain, it took in five large and eight small lakes, eight shrines for mountain pilgrims and a pine grove. Together, these make up a unique set of elements, linked by religious, historical and **esthetic**[5] traditions that can be summed up in the formula of a "sacred mountain."

Fuji's importance as a pilgrimage site is only half due to its status as Japan's tallest and handsomest volcano. Equally decisive is its position in sight of the capital. That could explain why Fuji pilgrimages reached their peak of popularity in the late Edo period, and among urban people. As commerce and business prospered, townspeople wanted to satisfy a need for more permanent, less material values. Today's trails from the gateway shrines to the summit were marked out in this period, and pilgrim networks were organized, with pilgrim fraternities building shrines and lodging houses and arranging ascents and spiritual training. Climbing for recreation arrived later, in the Meiji period, but never entirely replaced the pilgrimages. Today there is a curious blend, half recreational and half spiritual, with most people aiming to reach the top

Chapter 3 Mount Fuji: The Responsibilities of Heritage

just before sunrise in order to greet the "go-raiko" ("dayspring").

Urban pilgrims, then, are at the core of the image of Mount Fuji that has been registered as a world heritage property. And registration is not only a matter of the world recognizing this heritage, but also an undertaking by Japan to protect this image and to **restore**[6] parts of it that are in danger of being lost. In particular, Shizuoka and Yamanashi Prefectures have to prepare a revised plan by the end of 2016 to guide their future land use and management decisions.

One weakness that has to be repaired is that the history of the pilgrim routes on the lower parts of the mountain cannot easily be appreciated because of development masking the relationships between the routes and the shrines. Higher up, the huts and various other kinds of infrastructure serving the needs of modern pilgrims work against the spiritual atmosphere of the mountain. Responses to these problems will need to be included in the master plans followed by Shizuoka and Yamanashi Prefectures in their future management of the site.

The most delicate point, though, will be "visitor management." By the end of 2014, the two prefectures have to complete a joint visitor management strategy, which they will then follow when taking decisions about the capacities of the climbing routes, service buildings, and parking areas. The difficult question here is how to treat climbers. If they are Fuji "pilgrims," they are a living part of the tradition that the prefectures are working to protect. But if they are "visitors" in the usual management sense, their numbers may need limiting in order to protect the site and prevent overcrowding.

The number of climbers has risen recently, from 200,000 before 2005 to around 300,000 since 2008. After the UNESCO registration, over 400,000 were predicted for 2013, although in fact the figure stayed steady at 310,000. But car restrictions may have held it down, and it is possible that the rising trend will continue. There are already tailbacks up to the summit at peak times, and in bad weather these can be dangerous. In the summer of 2013, Shizuoka and Yamanashi Prefectures introduced a **voluntary**[7] contribution charge of ¥1,000 per person, which nearly everyone paid cheerfully. But the next problem was whether to make this charge **compulsory**,[8] and how high to set it — some people suggested an amount of ¥7,000, because a lower charge would not have much effect as a measure against crowding. But how would a ¥7,000 charge have squared with the story of Fuji the sacred mountain?

NOTES

UNESCO = United Nations Educational, Scientific and Cultural Organization「国連教育科学文化機関(ユネスコ)」 **the World Heritage Committee**「世界遺産委員会」 **the heritage site in the Kii Peninsula mountains**「紀伊半島山地にある遺産地域」世界文化遺産の紀伊山地霊場と参詣を指す。 **pine grove**「松林」三保の松原を指す。 **pilgrim fraternity**「講社」 **lodging house**「宿泊所」 **visitor management strategy**「訪問者管理戦略」

TRUE / FALSE

Mark these statements true (T) or false (F).

1. The first attempt to have Mount Fuji registered as a world heritage site was in 2013. [T / F]

2. The height and shape of Mount Fuji are totally different from those of any other mountains in the world. [T / F]

3. As a recent trend, single-feature sites are becoming less easy to register. [T / F]

4. A rise in ordinary people's prosperity helped boost the pilgrimages to Mount Fuji in the late Edo period. [T / F]

5. In today's management of the Fuji site, there is no need to think separately about people's recreational and spiritual motives for climbing. [T / F]

6. The number of climbers was expected to increase after the UNESCO registration. [T / F]

COMPREHENSION

Answer the questions in English.

1. What were the most widely reported reasons for giving up the attempt to have Mount Fuji recommended for registration in 2003?

2. What recent trend can be seen clearly in the Kii Peninsula mountains site?

3. What is meant by the phrase "more permanent and less material values"?

Chapter 3 Mount Fuji: The Responsibilities of Heritage

4. What sorts of things spoil the spiritual atmosphere on the higher parts of the mountain?

   _____

5. What is the difference between a visitor and a pilgrim?

   _____

GUIDED SUMMARY
CD1-13

Fill in the blanks with the words listed below.

Mount Fuji was approved for registration as a UNESCO world (1_____) heritage site in June 2013. Along with the mountain, the site takes in five large and eight small (2_____), eight shrines for mountain pilgrims and a pine grove. Fuji's growth as a (3_____) center was only half due to its status as a tall and handsome volcano. It was also attractive for its nearness to the major city of Tokyo. Urban pilgrims, in fact, are a core part of the reason for which Mount Fuji has been (4_____) as a world heritage site. Unfortunately, this (5_____) history of the pilgrim routes is not always evident around the lower parts of the mountain, while higher up, the huts and various other kinds of (6_____) for climbers work against the original spiritual atmosphere of the site.

| infrastructure | pilgrimage | background | registered | cultural | lakes |

COLUMN

　国連教育科学文化機関(UNESCO)が世界遺産制度を創設したのは1972年で、今では世界で190カ国が参加し、1,000件以上が世界遺産に登録されています。日本は1983年に法隆寺と姫路城、1984年に京都と宇治の神社仏閣が登録されたのが始まりです。これらはいずれも文化遺産です。それ以来、多くの文化遺産と自然遺産が指定されてきました。これまで世界遺産にさほど関心を示さなかった国々の姿勢が変わってきたのと歩調を合わせるかのように、世界遺産登録に向けての競争が激化するという事情がありそうです。
　文化遺産や自然遺産は世界全体で登録が1,000件以上になるにつれて、年々審査も厳しくなっていると報じられています。富士山も単なる自然遺産ではなく、古来の信仰と併せて文化遺産に申請し直したという戦略が功を奏したと考えられます。地元では、世界遺産登録によって観光客が増えるという期待が高まっています。

Tasty Vegetables: How much Extra would you Pay for them?

CHAPTER 4

　今世紀に入って、有機野菜など安全性に着目した食品に対する関心が高まっています。日本では生活協同組合（生協）を通じて、そのような食品を購入して宅配してもらうことが主流です。値段は量販店で買うよりも割高ですが、生産者の顔写真を公開するなどして購買者が安心できるような仕組みを整えています。英国や米国での動きも見ておきましょう。

生協宅配で用いられる容器

VOCABULARY

Match these expressions from the text with the items closest in meaning in the box below.

(1) ingredient ___   (2) affordable ___   (3) recruit ___
(4) convergence ___   (5) initiative ___   (6) municipality ___
(7) middleman ___   (8) trade-off ___

> a. gather people for a purpose   b. food item used in a recipe   c. balancing of values
> d. coming together into the same pattern   e. independent plan   f. city or town
> g. merchant who buys things to sell to others   h. not too expensive

16

Chapter 4 Tasty Vegetables: How much Extra would you Pay for them?

READING CD1-14

   This may come as a shock to some readers, but as a fact of life to others: in a growing number of households, people no longer shop for vegetables but have them delivered, generally once a week. They arrive in a box containing up to a dozen different sorts. The householder puts them in the fridge and folds the box flat to be returned when the next delivery is made. Sometimes fruit is included as well, and there may be additional options like meat, eggs, cooking oil, meal kits with cooking instructions, or **ingredients**[1] for seasonal specialties such as New Year *o-sechi*. But vegetables are the staple item, and this kind of delivery may go by a name like "yasai set" or "yasai box." In British English, too, people talk now of "vegetable boxes," or "veg boxes." Nearly always, the vegetables are organically grown, or at least grown using less chemical fertilizer and insecticide than is usual with store food.

   Convenient delivery is nothing new, of course. Grocers offered it 100 years ago, and even shopping malls have rediscovered it now in response to competition from online shopping. Other reasons for not going to stores are not new, either. Unlike some shops, the Japanese cooperative movement "Seikyo" traditionally always tried to supply its members with goods which, on balance, were **affordable**,[2] safe and healthy, fair to producers and consumers, and deliverable anywhere. In places without an existing delivery point, members could have one created by **recruiting**[3] a sufficient number of fellow customers. But even in the Co-op, this old concept of vans stopping at fixed places has recently given way to online orders and home deliveries. Both in the commercial malls and in the more socially inspired Co-op, then, some **convergence**[4] is taking place with the growing new trend of veg boxes. CD1-15

   In America, a more direct model of cooperation in food sales has grown up under the name of "community-supported agriculture." Here, the idea is that local consumers agree to buy food regularly from local producers at rates that are lower than store price but still leave the growers with more for their produce. Again, other considerations of health, freshness, fairness and so on are also important for the buyer, so that in the end the cost may be higher than at stores, but the buyer accepts this because of the higher quality. And again, the delivery may be in the form of a "veg box," although that name is not used much in the U.S.A.

Both in Britain and America, if you look up sales plans like these on the Internet you will find attractive stories of farmers who stopped collaborating with big agribusiness to sell responsibly grown produce at fair prices to local people. One firm with a story that reads attractively in this way is Riverford, the second largest supplier of veg boxes in the U.K. On the company's website, the founder tells at some length how he "set up the veg box scheme in 1993, delivering to 20 local friends and families."

Successful start-ups of this sort expanded with the organic foods boom in the 2000s. Riverford, for example, built up a partnership of "sister farms" which now deliver all over Britain. According to the U.K. Soil Association report of 2013, organic veg box sales increased right through the economic crisis following 2008, and in 2012 accounted for 10.6 percent of U.K. organic food sales, up from 8.1 percent in 2008. The main reason customers gave for having produce delivered this way was because they found it healthy. The second and third reasons were environmental concern and freshness.

In Japan, this kind of growth probably still lies in the future. There are already plenty of **initiatives**[5] for promoting local produce, supported by **municipalities**,[6] NPOs or producer networks, and direct sale markets are found everywhere, even in highway rest areas. But there is not yet much labeling of the conditions under which produce is grown. And although veg boxes may be increasing, they do not yet present a much greater challenge to the shopping malls than Co-op deliveries did before them.

For now, it looks as if organic veg boxes remain a controlled market under the umbrella of national-scale suppliers like Radish Boya and Oisix. These firms differ in their organic control standards, but offer more transparency than elsewhere at prices that are higher than for store veg but lower than for organic produce in stores. It can certainly be said that they offer a secure roof for small producers in search of regular sales. But the removal of the profit-taking **middleman**[7] is not their primary interest. For the customer, finally, the information about the supplied vegetables along with the recipe tips in each box make fascinating reading, no matter how the **trade-off**[8] works out between quality of life and price.

Chapter 4 Tasty Vegetables: How much Extra would you Pay for them?

NOTES

co-op = cooperative 「生活協同組合」 **veg box scheme** 「野菜ボックス」配達による販売方法(英国での呼び方) **sister farm** 「姉妹農園」業務提携で有機野菜などを栽培する。 **the Soil Association** 「英国土壌協会」有機農業などを推進する慈善団体。1973年に有機農産物の基準を決め、その設定をしている。**rest area** 「高速道路休憩所」売店や食事処が併設されていることが多い。 **Radish Boya, Oisix** 「らでぃっしゅぼーや」「おいしっくす」ともに有機野菜・低農薬野菜、無添加食品の宅配サービスを行う日本企業

TRUE / FALSE

Mark these statements true (T) or false (F).

1. Veg boxes contain vegetables grown with more chemical fertilizers than those in usual stores. [T / F]

2. Delivering food direct to households is a revolutionary new idea. [T / F]

3. In the U.S.A., people can buy better-quality vegetables through consumer-supported agriculture than they can in stores. [T / F]

4. For some farmers, direct sales have been a responsible way of breaking their ties with agribusiness. [T / F]

5. Organic veg box sales in the U.K. stopped increasing after the economic crisis in 2008. [T / F]

6. In Japan, direct sales of local produce are not likely to increase any more. [T / F]

COMPREHENSION

Answer the questions in English.

1. How frequently are veg and fruit boxes delivered to households?
   _____

2. How has the tradition of Co-op van sales changed recently?
   _____

3. When did the really big boom in organic foods occur?
   _____

4. What was the top reason named by U.K. consumers for having veg boxes delivered?
   _____

5. What fascinating reading materials are often provided along with veg boxes?

   _____

GUIDED SUMMARY   CD1-17

Fill in the blanks with the words listed below.

In a growing number of ($_1$_____), people are having fresh vegetables and fruits delivered direct to the door. The produce is often ($_2$_____) grown, or grown using less chemical ($_3$_____). The deliveries are in the form of so-called ($_4$_____), which generally come about once a week. In the U.S.A., a more direct model of cooperation has developed between farmers and local ($_5$_____). By not selling through ($_6$_____), the farmers are able to provide healthier produce cheaply and still make a profit.

> organically   middlemen   veg boxes   households   consumers   fertilizer

COLUMN

　英国と日本は、国土の広さや生協運動などで共通点が多そうです。日本の生協運動は、欧州を手本として始まったと考えられるでしょう。世界最大規模の組合員165万人を擁するコープ神戸の前身は、1921年に設立されています。生協が設置されている大学も多くあります。生協は組合という組織で、組合員だけが利用できるというのが特徴です。

　他方で国土の広い米国は、流通一つを取っても英国や日本とは大きく異なるでしょう。また、有機栽培とは対照的な遺伝子組み換え（GM）作物で世界で最も進んでいる国といえるでしょう。効率や安さを目指してGM作物のような方向に進むのか、安心して口にできる食べ物を目指す生協運動を進めるのか――文明論の対立といえるかもしれません。

Can Cars Drive themselves? And who is to Blame when they Crash?

CHAPTER 5

　自動運転車の技術が実用に近づいているようです。画像認識とその解析・処理能力が向上したことにより、安全性が格段に良くなりました。自動車メーカー各社は、電気自動車の開発と併せてしのぎを削っています。これからの課題は、事故が起こった際に責任を誰が負うかという点です。車に乗っている人が責任を負わなければ、その責めは自動車メーカーに課せられるでしょう。

自動運転を実験しているトラック

VOCABULARY

Match these expressions from the text with the items closest in meaning in the box below.

(1) accelerate ___ (2) legislation ___ (3) crosswalk ___ (4) negligence ___
(5) coast around ___ (6) jerky ___ (7) revert ___ (8) liability ___

a. glide around	b. pedestrian crossing	c. rough	d. increase speed
e. law making	f. abandonment of responsibility		g. change back
h. responsibility			

21

READING

It certainly made a publicity splash for the 2013 Tokyo Motor Show when Prime Minister Shinzo Abe was taken on trips around the Diet Building in self-driving cars made by Toyota, Honda and Nissan. "I felt with my own body that Japanese technology is the world's best," he said. This was the first time driverless cars had run on ordinary public roads, as distinct from expressways, in Japan. But Abe could not go quite as far as to call it a world premiere.

Autonomous vehicles, as they are more technically called, had been out in public a few years already. The DARPA Challenge for driverless cars in California began as a road race in 2004, and in 2007 it was changed to a different format in which cars needed to follow traffic rules and react to other vehicles. Trials in ordinary traffic began around 2010. One eye-catching example started from Rome, when the Artificial Vision and Intelligent Systems Laboratory at the University of Parma sent several small electric vans on a three-month, 90 percent driverless journey to the Shanghai Expo.

But perhaps the most publicized trials in town traffic were run by Google in the San Francisco Bay area, again starting in 2010. These used Toyota cars, so in that sense Abe's pride in Japan's contribution may have been justified. By May 2012, 500,000 miles (800,000 km) had been covered, and according to early data the cars braked and **accelerated**[1] more smoothly than with human drivers and maintained safer distances from other vehicles. Road trials of this kind will develop further. At present, there has to be a human operator in the car ready to take over if anything goes wrong. But in Nevada in 2011, a new law was approved to permit vehicles to run completely driverless under certain strict conditions. Other states, including California, have now prepared similar laws, and **legislation**[2] has also been passed in the U.K. and Sweden.

Naturally, the question of which style of driving is safer also involves other considerations than distances and pedal responses. How "safe" a vehicle is depends on what sort of safety is meant. For a human driver coming upon someone standing confused on a **crosswalk**,[3] the only really safe behavior is to stop and help the person off the road. In some countries, anything else would be criminal **negligence**.[4] But for a self-driving car, an optimal solution might be to **coast** safely **around**[5] the person without any **jerky**[6] braking.

Different ideas of what makes good driving can appear in other ways as

Chapter 5 Can Cars Drive themselves? And who is to Blame when they Crash?

well. For example, the Swedish car maker Volvo has been researching into the advantages of safety and efficiency that would come from unmanned trucks traveling down highways in intercommunicating groups informing and directing each other — like social networkers on wheels. This might suit freight logistics but not the owners of ordinary self-driving cars, whose movements would need to adapt to the ways of the networking trucks. Even in a self-driving car, an individual road user has different interests from a freight company, whose chief concern is punctual reliability. One point that is clear is that the individual will expect an escape option. That is to say, there will need to be a choice of **reverting**[7] back to a more independent and less directed mode of driving when that is what the driver wants.

Optimal solutions for everyone will be arrived at eventually through give and take. But in the meantime, it is hard for anyone to predict what level of autonomous driving is best for this or that sort of road user, or for road use as a whole. Early road trials can only measure the technical capabilities out of which future solutions will be born.

Another thing that also needs thinking about, because it clashes with some people's common sense, is the question of accident **liability**.[8] Returning to the confused person on the crosswalk: If the occupant of the self-driving car does nothing to help and a following vehicle then knocks the pedestrian down, how is the responsibility for the accident to be shared? How far is the occupant of the first car at fault for trusting to the self-driving system and not helping positively? The question needs to be asked because, no matter how safe these systems are, this sort of accident is really going to happen.

In the past, when an accident was caused by a function beyond a driver's knowledge or control, it was easy to assign responsibility to the manufacturer. But in the new world of autonomous vehicles, the distinction between "how the vehicle failed" and "how the vehicle occupant failed to control the vehicle" may become less sharp, and may also provide less protection for the vehicle owner.

NOTES

the Diet Building　「国会議事堂」　**DARPA** = the Defense Advanced Research Projects Agency 「国防高等研究計画局」先端技術を研究する米国防総省の機関　**Parma**　「パルマ」イタリア北部の都市　**the Shanghai Expo**　「上海万博」中国の最大都市である上海で2010年に開催された万国博覧会。1970年開催の大阪万博入場者数記録を40年ぶりに更新し，7,000万人超が来場した。

TRUE / FALSE

Mark these statements true (T) or false (F).

1. In 2013, the prime minister was driven around the Tokyo Motor Show in three Japanese self-driving cars. [T / F]

2. The DARPA challenge became less of a simple road race in 2007. [T / F]

3. Self-driving cars are able to run more smoothly than human-driven ones. [T / F]

4. For unmanned trucks, there will be advantages in sharing information. [T / F]

5. With autonomous vehicles, responsibility for accidents will become easier to assign. [T / F]

6. After autonomous driving becomes widespread, accidents will no longer happen. [T / F]

COMPREHENSION

Answer the questions in English.

1. What is a more technical name for self-driving cars?

   _____

2. How good was the braking and accelerating performance of the driverless cars in the Google road trials?

   _____

3. What is the safest thing to do when you see a person standing in the middle of a crosswalk and looking confused?

   _____

4. What is a freight company's chief concern for its long-distance truck shipments?

   _____

5. How has liability usually been assigned for accidents due to car design functions?

   _____

Chapter 5　Can Cars Drive themselves? And who is to Blame when they Crash?

GUIDED SUMMARY　　　　　　　　　　　　　　　　CD1-21

Fill in the blanks with the words listed below.

We are now on the point of entering a new age of (1_____) cars or, to put it more (2_____), autonomous vehicles. Vehicles without drivers are already in use in some workplaces, but in the past ten years public road (3_____) have also been taking place. Previously, this has only been allowed if a human driver is in the vehicle to take over in emergencies, but (4_____) is now being passed to allow totally unmanned vehicles on public roads under certain (5_____) conditions. The ultimate legal difficulty with autonomous driving is deciding where to assign (6_____) if something totally unpredictable happens and leads to an accident.

technically	strict	legislation	liability	trials	self-driving

COLUMN

　時代はアナログからデジタルへ——自動車の世界にも、この波は確実に及んでいます。家電製品では、アナログ時代のテレビはソニーなど日本製が優位に立っていました。しかしデジタル時代に移行して品質に差がなくなり、価格競争で日本企業は後れを取ってしまいました。自動車では、蓄電池とモーターの性能で同様の競争が懸念されます。高性能のモーターや電池が開発されれば、世界の自動車業界は勢力図が一変するかもしれません。

　自動運転という分野も、未知の技術であるだけに多様な可能性を秘めているといえるでしょう。この分野は画像認識や処理というような技術が事故を回避するための方策に直結するだけに、幅広い部門の総合力が試されそうです。

Germany's Departure from Nuclear Energy

CHAPTER 6

　東日本大震災に伴って福島第１原子力発電所が事故を起こした直後、ドイツは当初の2030年までに原発を全廃するという方針を早めて、8年前倒しにすることを決めました。この決定に至るには今世紀初頭の6年間、環境保護政策を訴える緑の党が連立政権に加わっていた影響が大きいといえます。ドイツでは原子力依存のエネルギー政策を見直し、風力や太陽光など再生可能エネルギーへの転換を目指しています。

上空から眺めたドイツの発電所

VOCABULARY

Match these expressions from the text with the items closest in meaning in the box below.

(1) rigorous ___　(2) conform to ___　(3) refit ___　(4) coalition ___
(5) resonate ___　(6) spectrum ___　(7) insulation ___　(8) decentralized ___

a. joint government	b. be widely heard	c. not controlled from the center
d. avoidance of electricity loss	e. complete range	f. match
g. change the equipment in a system	h. strict	

26

Chapter 6 Germany's Departure from Nuclear Energy

READING

Even before the accident at Fukushima, there was reluctance in Japan to provide new sites for nuclear plants to replace first-generation ones nearing the end of their 40-year lifetime. In the end, the government began extending their service lives. The same was happening in other advanced countries: Germany in 2010, France in 2012, Taiwan, Britain and Spain in 2014. The Nuclear Energy Institute, representing the U.S. power plant industry, now argues that an 80-year service life is safe, provided a responsible "life extension program" is followed. With this development, the debate around Fukushima appears to be moving from: "Can we afford nuclear power?" to: "No life extensions without a responsible program."

After its nuclear switch-off, Japan is getting ready to rejoin this trend. The more **rigorous**[1] inspection standards announced after the accident were more than just emergency reactions. They also **conform to**[2] the international strategy of **refitting**[3] and relicensing at least some of the first-generation installations instead of replacing them.

There is one country, however, which reacted more radically to the Fukushima accident than Japan did and is showing no sign of weakening its stance. Germany had 17 nuclear plants in 2011, but decided to shut eight of them and phase out the rest by 2022. To make up for this, it would increase the share of renewable energies (wind, photovoltaic, etc.) in power generation from 20 percent in 2011 to 50 percent by 2030, and 80 percent by 2050. Total consumption of energy would also drop 20 percent by 2030, and 50 percent by 2050.

In effect, Germany was returning to a nuclear exit policy it had already adopted in 2002. The exit date had subsequently been extended to 2030, but surveys after Fukushima showed that 90 percent of the population favored the 2022 schedule. In Japan, the government was also reacting to public opinion; but opinions about energy and the environment in Germany have a different history.

A sign of this is the existence of the Green Party, which was in government from 2002 to 2008 in **coalition**[4] with the Social Democrats. The party's website slogan is "Germany is renewable. We are ready for the green transformation," a message that **resonates**[5] far beyond the circle of their voters. In 2002, the party's price for joining the coalition was a policy initiative called the "Energiewende" ("energy turn-around"), from the title of an alternative energy report *Energiewende: Growth and Prosperity without Petroleum and Uranium* (1980) which outlines a strategy for a change to safer and more sustainable energy resources.

The core of this strategy is the ambitious changeover to renewable energies that was mentioned above. In Germany, the most promising renewable power source is wind, especially from the North Sea; but a **spectrum**[6] of photovoltaic, geothermal, hydro and biomass sources is required. The reason this kind of power is often considered insufficient for national needs is because engineers think in terms of large plants. But a lot of generating can be done on a small scale. Solar roof panels are a familiar example.

Once every locality is regarded as a potential generating site, what remains is to add grid storage and supply lines. This makes stored power available for where and when it is needed. Power generated at night can be stored for the daytime, and power from rural areas can be sent to the cities. Finally, tying this together requires improved **insulation**,[7] smart sharing capacities, and a higher integration of household, office and industrial energy uses. In a word, the energy grid needs to become as **decentralized**[8] and instantaneous as the Internet already is.

There are drawbacks, of course. Infrastructure costs are high, and people must come to accept small energy facilities and power lines around their homes. Those who do not generate power at home will also end up paying more to benefit those who do. But the people who stand to lose most are the traditional power companies. As homes, offices and factories become more self-sufficient, these companies are already losing business. Some of them are moving over into a new growth sector: consultancy services for home, office and factory energy efficiency.

NOTES

first-generation 「第一世代の」原子力発電所は従来、稼働してから40年が寿命とされていた。
the Nuclear Energy Institute 「原子力エネルギー院」 **photovoltaic (energy)**「太陽光発電」
the Green Party 「緑の党」ドイツの環境政策重視政党 **the Social Democrats** 「社会民主党」ドイツの中道左派政党 ***Energiewende*** 「エネルギー転換」石油と原子力によるエネルギーからの転換を提唱したドイツの政策提言 **hydro**「水力発電」 **biomass**「バイオマス」生物由来の有機性資源で、石油など化石資源を除いたもの

Chapter 6 Germany's Departure from Nuclear Energy

TRUE / FALSE

Mark these statements true (T) or false (F).

1. A change seems to be occurring in advanced countries away from plans to close down old nuclear power plants toward an extension of their service life. [T / F]

2. Germany is acting against the trend of allowing service-life extensions. [T / F]

3. "Petroleum" and "Uranium" in the subtitle of the *Energiewende* report refer to oil and nuclear power, respectively. [T / F]

4. Wind power alone would be a sufficient source of renewable energy in Germany. [T / F]

5. With renewable energies, a country can conveniently meet the demand for power at all times without any need for storage. [T / F]

6. In future, people who do not generate their own power at home will eventually have to pay more to benefit people who do. [T / F]

COMPREHENSION

Answer the questions in English.

1. What will be required for the service life of nuclear plants to be extended to 80 years?

   _____

2. What do you think the Green Party's slogan "Germany is renewable" means?

   _____

3. Why do engineers often think that renewable energies are insufficient for national needs?

   _____

4. In what ways will the energy grid of the future have to be more like the Internet?

   _____

5. How can traditional power companies survive this changeover to renewable energy?

   _____

GUIDED SUMMARY

Fill in the blanks with the words listed below.

As other countries are looking for ways to refit aging (1_____) power plants, Germany is bringing forward the (2_____) of its last nuclear plants from 2030 to an earlier target of 2022, as originally agreed under the (3_____) government of Social Democrats and Greens in 2002. Meeting this target will require a changeover from large plants burning fossil and nuclear fuels to smaller but more numerous ones based on (4_____) resources. A wide (5_____) of energy sources will have to be combined, including wind, photovoltaic, hydro, geothermal and biofuel. As a result, (6_____) power companies may find themselves in new roles as energy advisors and service providers.

coalition   spectrum   first-generation   closure   renewable   traditional

COLUMN

　福島第1原子力発電所の事故後、原子力発電所の寿命を延ばすか否かは国によって対応が別れているようです。ドイツのように早々と原発全廃を決めた国は少数です。フランスは全電力の7割を原子力で賄っていますが、オランド政権下でもこの比率を下げることには慎重であるように見受けられます。米国の原発依存度は約2割ですが、1979年のペンシルベニア州スリーマイル島原発の炉心溶融事故以来、30年以上も新規原発の建設は停止していました。

　原子力発電には、使用済み核の処理という難問題があります。原発でウランを燃やした後にはプルトニウムという元素が残りますが、英国やフランス、日本はこれを再処理して燃料として利用する方針です。しかしこの再処理はかえって費用がかかるという難点と技術が確立されていないという面があり、議論を複雑にしています。

CHAPTER 7

Lest the World Forget: History as Storytelling

国連教育科学文化機関（ユネスコ）が策定している世界遺産に「記憶遺産」という部門があります。日本で初めて記憶遺産に登録されたのが山本作兵衛氏が描いた炭鉱労働の実態です。このように「人類の記憶にとどめなければならない遺産」というのは、往々にして負の遺産という側面が大きいといえるかもしれません。それは「忘れてはならない」という意味であり、真実を知る語り部によって語り継がれなければならないとも言えるでしょう。

福岡県田川市に残る三井炭坑の伊田坑

VOCABULARY

Match these expressions from the text with the items closest in meaning in the box below.

(1) hardship ___ (2) traumatic ___ (3) marginalization ___ (4) expulsion ___
(5) attendant ___ (6) interpretation ___ (7) authentic ___ (8) profiteering ___

a. accompanying	b. true to reality	c. painful experience
d. reading of meaning	e. not allowing people a central role	
f. shocking and upsetting	g. forcing people out	h. making unfair profits

31

People nowadays are not satisfied with just seeing places where past events occurred. They want to interact with people who were there, or, if that is no longer possible, find people with good local knowledge of how things used to be. For towns and cities, it is becoming important to find residents who can respond to interests like these or, if necessary, to train them. In Japan, these narrators of the past are called *kataribe*, and in recent years their number has been increasing. Kataribe are wanted in numerous areas of life, but three especially frequent demands are for people who know about traditions or skills, people from certain occupational backgrounds, and people with first-hand experience of manmade or natural **hardships**.[1] Let us look at examples from each of these areas in turn.

One special example of narrating a local tradition can be found in Tono, Iwate Prefecture, where Kunio Yanagita once collected folk legends. Before going around to view the locations of these legends, visitors can call at a facility called the House of Tales to be told stories by a volunteer *kataribe*. Here, storytelling itself is the tradition being introduced and demonstrated. A more ordinary case would be a hands-on introduction to a local handcraft tradition such as pottery making, in an atmosphere that comes close to informal narrating.

A well-known early example of an occupational storyteller was Sakubei Yamamoto, who put his 50 years as a miner in the Chikuho coalfield in Kyushu into sketches that are now preserved in the Tagawa Coal Mining History Museum. He also put his experiences into talks, articles and TV documentaries. Long after his death, the museum still hosts small-audience narrating events at which retired miners talk about work and life as it once was in the region.

The third field of kataribe activity, recalling personal experiences of large-scale hardship, whether resulting from manmade or natural causes, is far more difficult to handle. In a "Newspapers in Education" supplement in August 2013, timed to coincide with the anniversary of the end of the Pacific War, one Japanese newspaper stressed the importance of the role of storytelling in keeping the memory of past sufferings alive. As examples, it introduced 25 local projects relating to sufferings in four categories of war, pollution, natural disasters and others. **Traumatic**[2] war experiences were at the center of 13 of these projects. Four others were concerned with pollution damage to health from the high growth era of the 1950s and 1960s. Three projects recalling natural disasters were all situated in the 1990s and took in a volcanic eruption, a tsunami, and an earthquake. The fourth, mixed category included social and political failures which are still not wholly faced up to: three cases of social **marginalization**³ involving *Buraku* families, Ainu culture, and Hansen disease patients and two wrongs arising out of Cold War power rivalry: the **expulsions**⁴ from the Northern Territories and the radiation fallout from the Bikini bomb tests.

Behind all of these projects, there is an uncomfortable feeling that living memories of the past will soon be lost. In Hiroshima City, for example, the remaining task of the storytellers who personally experienced the atom bomb is to train a follower generation of kataribe — people who were not there in 1945, but have access to "a good local knowledge."

Keeping projects running is one thing. But an equally challenging problem is how to open up a hardship experience for storytelling in the first place. There is always an **attendant**⁵ problem of "Who has the right of **interpretation**⁶ over other people's sufferings?" A hard case to judge at the moment is the tour activity surrounding the 2011 tsunamis. It comes as a shock at first to find terms like "kataribe bus tour" or "kataribe taxi" in travel advertisements. In the case of a bus tour advertised by one hotel in Minami Sanriku, the storyteller seems to be a hotel staff member, a fact which might initially raise suspicions. However, this hotel did serve as a tsunami relief center in 2011, so its staff may have an **authentic**⁷ story to tell. Also, the ¥500 tour fare does not look like commercial **profiteering**.⁸ Conducted with respect, a tour like this can certainly help to convey the region's sense of loss to outside visitors, at least until other storytellers are ready to take over on a more clearly independent basis.

A key question behind all this is: What is authenticity in storytelling? The answer cannot be factual truth, since legend sharing, as in the case of Tono, can also be authentic. It must be a matter of values. If your story is important to you and you want it to be important to your listener, in other words, if you are sharing something that really matters, your story is authentic.

NOTES

Kunio Yanagita 柳田国男（1875-1962）「日本民俗学の父」と称される。岩手県の民話を集めた『遠野物語』は代表作。　**Sakubei Yamamoto** 山本作兵衛（1892-1984）福岡県出身の炭鉱労働者。炭鉱労働の様子を描き、2011年に日本初の世界記憶遺産に登録された。　**the Chikuho coalfield**「筑

豊炭田」福岡県にあった炭田　**the Tagawa Coal Mining History Museum**「田川市石炭・歴史博物館」福岡県田川市に開設され、炭鉱の様子などを展示している。**the Northern Territories**「北方領土」北海道根室沖の歯舞諸島、色丹島、国後島、択捉島を指す。**the Bikini bomb tests**「ビキニ水爆実験」ビキニ環礁はフィリピン東方約4,000キロの太平洋上に位置するマーシャル諸島共和国にある。1946~58年に米国が水爆実験を行い、54年の実験で日本漁船の第5福竜丸が「死の灰」を浴びて乗組員が被曝した。

TRUE / FALSE

Mark these statements true (T) or false (F).

1. Today, people do not often feel like asking residents in an area about their knowledge and experience of the local past.　[T / F]

2. The House of Tales in Tono is a typical example of the narrating of a local handcraft tradition.　[T / F]

3. Narrations of mining experiences still continue at the Tagawa museum, long after Yamamoto's death.　[T / F]

4. It is not at all easy to arrange projects in which local people share their experiences of large-scale hardship.　[T / F]

5. The ¥500 fare for the bus tour in Minami Sanriku seems expensive.　[T / F]

6. Storytelling is authentic when the person doing it is trying to share important values.　[T / F]

COMPREHENSION

Answer the questions in English.

1. Why are people not satisfied with just seeing the places where events happened?

2. What two ways does the Tagawa museum use to tell about the work experience of people like Sakubei Yamamoto?

3. What task remains to be done in Hiroshima by storytellers who experienced the atom bomb but are now growing old?

4. Why are experiences of hardship often difficult to open up into material for storytelling?

Chapter 7 Lest the World Forget: History as Storytelling

5. If you saw a bus tour along the tsunami-struck Tohoku coast advertised as a "Kataribe Tour," would you have any positive or negative feeling about it? What kind of feeling?

_____

GUIDED SUMMARY   CD1-29

Fill in the blanks with the words listed below.

Storytelling based on local people's experiences is a way of keeping a region's memories (1_____). The stories may concern local (2_____) or skills, or they may reflect the (3_____) lives of workers. The most difficult regional memories to share are those that recall large-scale (4_____) such as the tsunamis that struck Tohoku in 2011. At first, it seems as if no one has the right to (5_____) other people's sufferings. But as people begin to share what was important for them in these traumatic events, the results gradually grow into an authentic regional memory that is of (6_____) to the people in the area, even if it is not exactly the same as the private memory kept by each person.

| interpret | traditions | value | alive | hardships | occupational |

COLUMN

　記憶遺産登録は1992年に始まり、2013年6月時点で299点が登録されています。フランス革命時の「人権宣言」や支倉常長らの「慶長遣欧使節関係資料」など中立的な資料も多く含まれますが、山本作兵衛の「炭鉱絵画」やナチス抑圧下のオランダで書かれた「アンネの日記」など苦しい時代の記憶も多く含まれています。これらは、東日本大震災に伴う津波被害などを後世に語り伝える語り部の役割と共通する面があるかもしれません。それは、人が生きていく上ではどうしても良い行いと悪い行いが混在するという摂理に起因するように思えてなりません。そのような「負の遺産」も正面から受け止め、客観的に捉えるのが歴史を学ぶということかもしれません。

Eel and Tuna: Tastes the Next Generation may never Know?

CHAPTER 8

　日本人にとってなじみの深かったマグロやウナギという魚類が、世界中で個体数が減少したことによって私たちの口に入りにくくなりつつあります。マグロは、卵から完全養殖する技術が確立されています。ウナギはどこで生まれて成長するのかが長い間の謎でしたが、サイパン島西方約350キロの海域で産卵されるということが最近分かりました。しかしまだマグロのような完全養殖は不可能です。すしブームが世界中に広がる中で、日本の魚食文化はどこまで理解されるのでしょうか。

ウナギの握りずし

VOCABULARY

Match these expressions from the text with the items closest in meaning in the box below.

(1) quota ___　(2) stabilize ___　(3) smuggle ___　(4) break up ___
(5) outlet ___　(6) bribe ___　(7) rampant ___　(8) temptation ___

a. import or export illegally	b. limit on the number
c. impulse to do something wrong	d. put a stop to　　e. point of sale
f. pay illegally for a favor　　g. become steady　　h. widespread and out of control	

Chapter 8 Eel and Tuna: Tastes the Next Generation may never Know?

READING

Japan prides itself on being a fish-eating nation, and for certain kinds of fish people are ready to spend a lot. This was especially evident in 2013, when two of the most prized species were in desperately short supply at the same time. The largest bluefin tuna at the Tsukiji fish market's New Year auction that year went for ¥155.4 million. Admittedly, that was a symbolic price, not a normal commercial one. But only a few weeks later, "glass eels," the threadlike gelatine creatures that grow into grilling eels, were selling at a regular market price of ¥3 million a kilo. A year later, the New Year's bluefin was "only " ¥7 million, and glass eels were down to ¥550,000 a kilo. But these prices still seem out of proportion to the taste or food value of the fish. They also invite overfishing and illegal trading, and this is the main reason why many conservation activists point to Japan's consumers as the number one threat to the species' long-term survival.

Many Japanese people find this accusation unfair. Statistically, Japan takes less than 30 percent of the world's tuna catch, while 99.8 percent of the eel eaten here is farmed. All true. Yet things are a bit more complex.

Japan's share of the total tuna catch may be less than a third, but the biggest tunas, the bluefins, do go to the sushi and sashimi market, most of which is in Japan. The common complaint that "Japan takes three-quarters of the catch" refers to the bluefins in the Atlantic, where populations are smaller than in the Pacific. Large-scale fishing of these Atlantic bluefins began in the 1960s, causing numbers to collapse first in the Western Atlantic in the 1980s and then in the Eastern Atlantic and Mediterranean in the 1990s. There are annual catch **quotas**[1] now, but the populations have only **stabilized**,[2] not recovered. In the Pacific, numbers seem to fall and recover in cycles, leading to jumps in price like the one in 2013, which add to the pressure to fish in the Atlantic.

Regarding eels, half of Japan's supply comes from China, Taiwan and elsewhere, where they are raised from glass eels. But where these come from is not crystal-clear. At the height of the Japanese shortage in 2013, there were reports of illegal netting and **smuggling**[3] around the world. Fish preservation officers who **broke up**[4] a netting operation in New Hampshire said that netters were paid $2,000 a pound for glass eels "destined for Asian markets, where they are nurtured until full grown then sold to restaurants and other **outlets**."[5]

Another smuggling story in Jakarta involved **bribes**[6] paid to customs officers. Kyodo News chose a headline: "Indonesian glass eel smuggling **rampant**[7] as stocks decline in Japan."

As for the argument that tuna and eel eating are a part of Japanese culture, it ignores the fact that enjoying these fish as delicacies is different from mass-marketing them in shopping malls and conveyor-belt sushi bars. This mass commerce is an innovation, not a tradition; and with similar patterns developing in South Korea and China, world consumption of Japanese eels, for example, jumped from under 40,000 tons in 1980 to 260,000 tons in 2010.

Most eels have been farm-raised since the 1970s, as the rise in supply would not have been possible any other way. The first tuna farms followed in the 1990s, in Australia, Mexico, and a string of Mediterranean countries from Spain to Turkey, as well as Japan. Tuna farm production in Japan rose from 4,000 to 10,000 tons between 2007 and 2011, and has stayed steady since then.

In theory, farming may help to stabilize market supply in years when catches decline or fishing is restricted. It also offers a market for fish that are too small for eating when caught, and one day it might even make sea fishing less necessary so that overfished areas can be left to recover again. For high-value fish like eel or tuna, farming looks like the answer to many problems.

But it is not without risks. Farming is a competitive business, and as we have already seen with eel farming, one way to secure more fish at times of shortage is to buy from illegal catchers. For tuna farmers, too, there will be **temptations**[8] to buy not just fish that are small, but ones that should never have been caught, because they have not yet spawned (produced eggs).

The best way to avoid this is by breeding fish right through their life cycle, from spawning (egg-laying) and birth up to adulthood. But this is not easy. Japanese eels spawn near the Marianas, and drift for a year as larvae before reaching Northeast Asia and turning into glass eels. As for newborn tuna, they need space and peace. In a tank, they often become hyperactive and die, or eat each other. Experimenters at the Fisheries Research Agency have now succeeded in breeding both sorts of fish from eggs, and Kinki University's fisheries research unit in Wakayama has even registered a brand name, "Kindai Tuna (Maguro)," and opened two restaurants for cultivated tuna. But survival rates are low.

Chapter 8 Eel and Tuna: Tastes the Next Generation may never Know?

It will be a while yet before life-cycle breeding for either eel or tuna becomes commercially attractive.

NOTES

the Tsukiji fish market「築地魚市場」東京・築地にある世界最大級の鮮魚卸売市場 **bluefin tuna**「クロマグロ, 本マグロ」 **glass eel**「シラスウナギ」ウナギの稚魚 **Kyodo News**「共同通信社」全国の新聞社などによって設立され、現在は一般社団法人 **conveyor-belt sushi bar**「回転ずし店」 **the Marianas**「マリアナ諸島」 **larvae** [láːviː, láːrvai]「(変態する動物の)幼生」単数形はlarva [láːrvə] **the Fisheries Research Agency**「水産総合研究センター(独立行政法人)」 **Kindai Tuna**「近大マグロ」近畿大学が世界で初めて卵からの完全養殖に成功したマグロのブランド名

TRUE / FALSE

Mark these statements true (T) or false (F).

1. The prices for bluefin tuna and glass eels were both exceptionally high in 2013.   [T / F]

2. Statistically, Japan takes most of the world's tuna catch.   [T / F]

3. A shortage of fish in Japan can lead to illegal netting and smuggling all over the world.   [T / F]

4. Farmed tuna production in Japan declined sharply between 2007 and 2011.   [T / F]

5. For future conservation, it is best to catch small tuna that have not yet produced eggs.   [T / F]

6. Life-cycle breeding is now commercially attractive for both tuna and eels.   [T / F]

COMPREHENSION

Answer the questions in English.

1. According to conservation activists, where does the biggest threat come from for populations of fish such as bluefin tuna and eels?

2. What sort of pattern seems to appear in bluefin numbers in the Pacific?

3. What relation is there between new patterns of commerce in Korea and China and the increase in the world consumption of Japanese eels?

4. Theoretically speaking, why would fish farming make sea fishing less necessary?

   _____

5. Why do newborn tuna need plenty of space and peace?

   _____

GUIDED SUMMARY CD1-33

Fill in the blanks with the words listed below.

Japan is admired for its (1_____) traditions, but current patterns of mass consumption pose a (2_____) to world stocks of tuna and eel. The more immediate danger is to the (3_____). Wild ones are very rare in Japan now, and 99.8 percent of the eel eaten here is farmed. But in 2013, even baby glass eels for farm rearing were in critically short supply. Glass eels were (4_____) at abnormally high prices, and illegal netting and (5_____) were rampant around the world. For tuna, a note of hope is that a successful technique of (6_____) breeding has now been developed. The survival rate of the farmed fish is not high yet, but as it improves it will become possible to supply sushi restaurants from this source.

| smuggling | threat | life-cycle | eels | fish-eating | selling |

COLUMN

　ウナギは江戸時代から庶民にとっては高嶺の花でした。海に囲まれた日本は、古くから魚食文化を発達させてきました。近年のすしブームは世界中に日本の魚食文化を伝えるとともに、各地で独自の発達を遂げています。アボカドを使った「カリフォルニア巻き」などは、その代表例といえるでしょう。

　毎年、正月早々に東京・築地市場で行われる生鮮マグロの初競りは注目を集めます。ご祝儀相場という側面もありますが、マグロ1本に1億5,000万円という値を付けたのは話題を集めるためという意図があったのでしょう。200キロ以上あるマグロでも、この値段では採算が合わないことでしょう。

CHAPTER 9

Still Applying to Join the Euro

　欧州単一通貨ユーロは1999年に導入され、2002年から現金の流通が始まり、順調な滑り出しとみられていました。ところが2010年に入って、ギリシアの粉飾財政が発覚して一挙に財政危機が表面化しました。ユーロ圏で単一通貨を用いてはいても、財政面には各国の主権が及ぶという矛盾が露呈したのです。このユーロ危機は数年を経て表面上は沈静化していますが、これからユーロ圏に加わろうとする予備群もあり先行きは予断を許しません。

フランクフルトの欧州中央銀行

VOCABULARY

Match these expressions from the text with the items closest in meaning in the box below.

(1) yield ___　(2) convergence ___　(3) steer ___　(4) deficit ___
(5) unemployment ___　(6) compensate for ___　(7) bailout ___　(8) pledge ___

a. moving closer together	b. direct	c. promise	d. lack of jobs
e. financial help in an emergency		f. additional gain	
g. earning less money than is spent		h. offset	

READING

Not long ago, the European Monetary Union — the "Eurozone" as the media call it — seemed to be splitting apart. While protesters in the southern countries were demanding social as well as economic solutions to the debt crisis, the governments of the northern countries, especially Germany, insisted that what the indebted members needed to do first was to control their spending and rebuild their finances.

The main disagreement was over "sovereign debt," which may need explaining. A sovereign state is one which controls its own affairs, and this requires money. One important way of attracting money is by selling government debt bonds on which interest is later returned. The percentage of interest on these bonds is called the **yield**,[1] and the percentage depends on the state's international financial rating.

Obviously, a financially secure country can obtain outside money more cheaply. For example, German government ten-year bonds in February 2014 only needed to offer a low yield of 1.62 percent, while the Portuguese government had to offer 4.82 percent, since there was a perceived risk of not getting all of the money back. At this time, around the end of the Eurozone crisis, this meant that money-raising through bonds was three times more expensive for Portugal than for Germany. At the height of the crisis, in January 2012, Portugal would have needed to offer 17 percent to find buyers at all. Ironically, too, many of these high-yield bonds would have been bought by German banks using money obtained more cheaply.

In theory, large differences of risk and yield should not occur in a currency area. You would not expect different yields on yen bonds in Honshu and Kyushu, for example. The reason this happened in the Eurozone is because the national governments still kept their financial independence. To avoid large differences, all E.U. countries (not only the ones in the Eurozone) relied on keeping their financial goals in **convergence**[2] by continuously **steering**[3] in the direction of the best-performing countries. Up until the world financial crisis, which started in late 2008, this seemed to work. But as the crisis grew worse, buried differences came to the surface.

The theory was that financial convergence could be assured through the Maastricht criteria, which were a key element of the plan to set up the euro. The main rules were that countries had to keep their debts and budget **deficits**[4] low and stay close to the best-performing countries in inflation and exchange rate stability. Only E.U. members passing these criteria would be admitted to the first group of euro countries in 2002, and future members would be put through similar tests. All of the 12 countries that chose to adopt the euro currency at this first stage passed, although it is doubtful now whether all of them should have been accepted. Of 13 new E.U. members since, six have also qualified for the euro group and joined it.

Passing may involve cuts in public spending, leading to hardships and **unemployment**.[5] But the stability of the euro currency appears to **compensate for**[6] this. Before long, the early hardships are offset by business and property booms and changes in lifestyle. At least, this was the pattern before 2008. But by the time Estonia qualified in 2009, recession had set in. Instead of a boom, unemployment shot up, and young people began leaving. For Latvia, hoping to join at the same time, things went even worse. Instead of qualifying for the euro, Latvia became one of the first E.U. countries to require a **bailout**.[7] It recovered enough to join the euro in 2014, but it was still suffering economically.

Similarly, Hungary and Romania also needed help, but as they are not in the euro system yet, the media treated the crisis in a simpler way, as a story of the South of Europe, e.g. Greece and Portugal, demanding support from the North, especially Germany. In reality, the problems are more widespread, with 20 or so weaker economies struggling to keep pace with a core group of more powerful ones, from whom they also need to borrow. This time, it is a fact that the biggest bailouts were needed in the older E.U. member states Greece (€245 billion), Portugal (€78 billion), Ireland (€67 billion) and Spain (€41 billion). But the suspicion remains that the younger E.U. members have simply had fewer years in which to build up bond debts or property bubbles.

The Eurozone crisis was brought to a head in September 2012, when the president of the European Central Bank **pledged**[8] unlimited support for countries involved in bailout programs. Tighter lending controls were also imposed on banks, which could be the beginning of a more definite financial code. The measures apparently worked. Nobody did anything this time to put the pledge to an ultimate test of strength.

NOTES

the European Monetary Union「欧州通貨同盟」 **sovereign debt** 「政府債務」 **the Maastricht criteria** 「マーストリヒト基準」欧州連合条約(マーストリヒト条約)に基づく各国の財政基準。加盟各国の単年度財政赤字を対国内総生産(GDP)比3％以内に、政府債務残高を同60％以内に抑制することが定められている。**property bubble** 「不動産バブル」**the European Central Bank (ECB)** 「欧州中央銀行」ドイツのフランクフルトに本部が置かれ、ユーロ圏の物価安定を最大の課題として金融政策を決定する。

TRUE / FALSE

Mark these statements true (T) or false (F).

1. There was a lot of disagreement among E.U. countries about how to deal with the debt crisis. [T / F]

2. When a country has a strong financial rating, it offers a higher yield on its government debt bonds. [T / F]

3. Banks in financially stable countries can earn additional money by trading in the high-yield national bonds of countries such as Portugal. [T / F]

4. After the start of the world financial crisis, the convergence policy in the European Union continued to function just as well as before. [T / F]

5. Estonia and Latvia were able to join the Eurozone at the same time. [T / F]

6. The world media talked too much about "North-South" differences, when actually the debt crisis was also severe in eastern E.U. countries. [T / F]

COMPREHENSION

Answer the questions in English.

1. If the financial rating of Germany were to fall, what change would this lead to in the low yield rate of German national bonds?

   _____

2. Why do such large differences of risk and yield occur among countries using the same euro currency?

   _____

Chapter 9 Still Applying to Join the Euro

3. How do member countries of the E.U. try to keep their financial goals in convergence?

   _____

4. What were the four main conditions set out in the Maastricht criteria for countries preparing to change to the euro currency?

   _____

5. At first, changing to the euro involves hardships. How is this compensated later?

   _____

GUIDED SUMMARY   CD1-37

Fill in the blanks with the words listed below.

The European Monetary Union started in 1999, and the (1 _____) currency began to circulate in 2002. At that stage, 12 countries adopted it, but it is not clear that all of them satisfied the (2 _____). At first, there were property booms and signs of rapid (3 _____) in the weaker member countries. But after the start of the 2008 world financial crisis, it soon became (4 _____) that some countries had hidden debt problems. In Ireland and Spain banks ran into trouble, while in Greece and Portugal the governments themselves fell so badly into (5 _____) that they became unable to borrow money by offering new national (6 _____) at realistic yield rates.

| debt | growth | bonds | euro | criteria | obvious |

COLUMN

　ユーロ危機の発端は、ギリシアでの政権交代によって政府財政の粉飾が明らかになったことでした。最終的に13.6％と修正された国内総生産 (GDP) 比の財政赤字を、前政権は3.7％と偽っていたのです。2009年暮れのことでした。年が明けてから外国為替相場でユーロが暴落します。危機前は1ユーロが170円に迫った相場が、110円台にまで下がりました。本文でも指摘したように、ユーロ導入によってギリシアやポルトガルなど財政基盤が脆弱な国も低金利で国債が発行できるようになっていたのが原因です。

　2014年3月時点で、これからユーロ圏に入る予定があるのはブルガリア、チェコ、ハンガリー、ポーランド、ルーマニアの5カ国です。

Female Athletes Dramatized

CHAPTER 10

男女の差異は社会のさまざまな面に見られます。運動競技においても競技寿命や収入の差など、あらゆる面で男女差は存在します。この章では、フィギュアスケートの浅田真央選手とレスリングの吉田沙保里選手を比べてみます。フィギュアスケートとレスリングという競技の違いから、どのような運動能力が求められるかなどについては当然異なってきます。

女子走り高跳び

VOCABULARY

Match these expressions from the text with the items closest in meaning in the box below.

(1) stocky ___ (2) agility ___ (3) prodigy ___ (4) complementary ___
(5) cadet ___   (6) garb ___   (7) pep ___   (8) zany ___

a. outfit	b. compact and strongly built	c. a person of amazing ability
d. crazy, not at all normal	e. energy, an active spirit	f. well matching
g. quickness in movement	h. junior	

Chapter 10 Female Athletes Dramatized

READING

Sports careers are rarely equal for men and women. Earnings are different, and women usually retire earlier. But that is not all. Even at the peak of their careers, female athletes are often not followed for their achievements alone. Rather, there are attempts to inject drama into the story. Consider the cases of the women who came first and second in the Oricon popularity ranking for female athletes in 2013: Mao Asada the figure skater and Saori Yoshida the freestyle wrestler.

Since Oricon, the music charts company, began rankings for athletes in 2007, Mao Asada (five times top, once second) has been almost constantly at the top of the women's table. Below her, there are athletes who appear and quickly fade, but also some who remain for years. Saori Yoshida is one of these stayers. But she is unusual in the way her popularity has gone on rising from tenth after her second Olympic gold in 2008, to ninth in 2010, eighth in 2011, fourth after a third gold in 2012, and second in 2013. This gradual ascent needs explaining.

Asada and Yoshida are different in some obvious ways. Asada is tall and slender, and Yoshida short and **stocky**.[1] But in speed, **agility**,[2] leg strength and coordination, they have a lot in common. Asada has the strength to perform typical male jumps, while Yoshida, for a wrestler, is a light-weight, relying greatly on her sharp reflexes.

It is difficult to compare their personal backgrounds without dropping into stereotypes. But in media reports they are both represented as having been introduced to sport by ambitious parents (Asada's mother, Yoshida's father). They were both youth **prodigies**[3] (Asada by the age of 14, Yoshida immediately), and so trained to succeed that they are said to have trouble dealing with failure — although this may be media exaggeration.

The greatest difference in early upbringing may have been that unlike Yoshida, Asada and her older sister Mai were introduced to the two **complementary**[4] disciplines of ballet and skating. Her sister's name means "dance," and her own name, Mao, is said to come from the Takarazuka and musical artist Mao Daichi. This early foundation in dancing helps to explain the sureness of grace and flow that characterizes Asada's skating programs. In addition to her powerful jumps, she was known early on for her Biellmann spin figures, in which she could spread her arms back to clasp a leg curved perfectly over her head.

This perfection is sometimes said to be Asada's undoing. She performs so close to the edge between the possible and the impossible that she sometimes ends with a technical error where a less perfect figure might have been enough for a win. In the 2014 Winter Olympics, the technical difficulty of her skating was outstanding, but while she succeeded completely with the free-skate program, she faulted badly in the short program and announced soon afterward that she was taking a year out from major competitions. But the public, it seems, appreciates her bids at perfection and stays as loyal to her when success just passes her by as when she manages to grasp it.

CD1-40

Yoshida's field of perfection is more concentrated: reading an opponent's reflex an instant before it is transmitted into action. Yoshida began training at age three in her father's wrestling school, and has reportedly never looked back. As of early 2014, she still has a perfect individual competition record since winning her first **cadet**[5] world championship in 1998. She has never won anything below gold, and has lost only two matches in team events. Strangely enough, she does not hold the record for an unbroken run of wins. That belongs to Kaori Icho, whose career record is almost identical to Yoshida's, but in the next weight class up.

Why Yoshida, rather than Icho, has struck such a chord with the public is hard to say. Part of it may be on account of her physical shortness. Although obviously powerful, she depends on speed and poise as Ryoko Tani once did in judo. Also, like Tani, she overwhelmingly projects positiveness. But another part of her strength, always in reserve, is humor. This can be seen in the way she has adapted to the ALSOK Home Security commercials. Originally, these compared the endurance of security guards with the rigorous training runs of a judo fighter, Kosei Inoue. But after Yoshida joined the squad in 2006, her red wrestling **garb**[6] lifted the series out of ordinary sports training into something more like a fantasy epic of superheroes patrolling the nation, restoring **pep**[7] to the spirits of hardworking local people, or at times crouching ninja-like in the angle between a wall and a ceiling ready to protect elderly households against all manner of intrusion or threat.

Things as **zany**[8] as this are seldom done with male athletes in commercials. Whether it is refreshing, or some kind of subtle paternalism, is not easy to decide.

Chapter 10 Female Athletes Dramatized

NOTES

the Oricon popularity ranking for female athletes「オリコン（9ページの註を参照）女子運動選手人気ランキング」 **Mao Daichi** 大地真央（1956-）宝塚歌劇団出身の女優 **Biellmann spin**「ビールマンスピン」片脚で回転し、もう片方の脚を背後から伸ばして頭上に高く持ち上げ、そのスケート刃を手でつかむ。 **Kaori Icho** 伊調馨（1984-）女子レスリング選手 **Ryoko Tani** 谷亮子（1975-）元柔道選手で参議院議員 **ALSOK Home Security**「綜合警備保障」ALSOKはAlways Security OKの意。 **Kosei Inoue** 井上康生（1978-）元柔道選手で、2000年シドニー五輪で金メダルを獲得。

TRUE / FALSE

Mark these statements true (T) or false (F).

1. Mao Asada has always held first place in the Oricon ranking for female athletes since it started in 2007. [T / F]

2. Asada and Yoshida are similar in their body types and athletic abilities. [T / F]

3. When people compare the personal backgrounds of athletes, there is a danger of falling into stereotypes. [T / F]

4. In the 2014 Winter Olympics, Asada at last won the gold medal. [T / F]

5. Yoshida's strengths are speed and poise rather than physical power. [T / F]

6. The ALSOK commercials became more humorous and imaginative after Yoshida joined the squad. [T / F]

COMPREHENSION

Answer the questions in English.

1. What does it mean "to inject drama into the story" (line 4)?

2. What has been unusual about Saori Yoshida's Oricon ranking?

3. Where does Mao Asada's sense of grace and flow seem to come from?

4. Why is Asada's perfection sometimes said to be her undoing?

5. What is Yoshida's particular field of perfection?
_____

GUIDED SUMMARY   CD1-41

Fill in the blanks with the words listed below.

The (1_____) Mao Asada is one of Japan's best loved sportswomen. She has been at the top of the women athletes' ranking for years. The freestyle wrestler Saori Yoshida, on the other hand, has risen in the rankings (2_____). The two are different in height and weight, but similar in their (3_____) of movement. As for (4_____), everyone admires Asada's grace, but some people find her performance goals too perfect. Yoshida more openly displays (5_____), as can be seen in her side job since 2006: appearing in zany TV (6_____) for a home security firm.

| figure skater | humor | personality | commercials | gradually | agility |

COLUMN

　一見華やかそうな女子スポーツですが、競技によって見る側の印象も随分と違ってくるのではないでしょうか。柔道やレスリングなどの格闘技、卓球やバレーボールのような球技、陸上や水泳、フィギュアスケートのような冬季種目——それぞれに求められる身体特性も異なります。
　フィギュアスケートと共通点が多そうなのは体操でしょうか。跳躍や回転という求められる身体能力も共通点が多いでしょうし、演技の滑らかさや芸術性など見た印象が左右する側面も共通しているといえそうです。

Islands of Safety – or Baby Hatches?

CHAPTER 11

　日本でも「赤ちゃんポスト」として有名になった新生児・乳児預託施設は、12世紀の欧州にまで起源をさかのぼります。ドイツでは最初に預けてから8週間の「考慮期間」があり、その期間中に赤ちゃんを引き取ることもできます。中国でも近年、似たような施設が設けられましたが、匿名で子を託すことができるので預けっぱなしになってしまうという違いがあります。

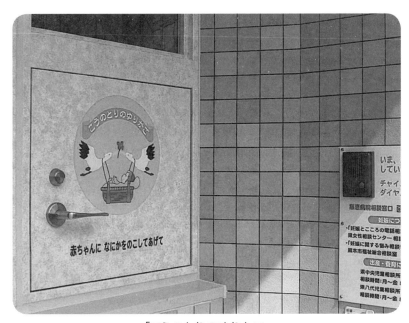

「こうのとりのゆりかご」

VOCABULARY

Match these expressions from the text with the items closest in meaning in the box below.

(1) incubator ___　　(2) quarantine ___　　(3) intervene ___
(4) publicity ___　　(5) intriguing ___　　(6) designated ___
(7) anonymously ___　(8) commemorative ___

a. release of information	b. interesting and curious	c. protective bed for a baby
d. without telling one's name	e. officially fixed	f. performed in memory of something
g. isolation to stop spread of disease	h. step in and influence	

In March 2014, there was an embarrassing problem with a "baby hatch" in Guangzhou, Guangdong Province, China. At least, "baby hatch" was the name widely used in the international media. The official Chinese name means literally an "island of safety for infants." The first one in China opened in 2011, in Shijiazhuang, Hebei Province. It is an air-conditioned shelter outside a home for orphans and abandoned children. It is open 24 hours a day, and houses a baby **incubator**.[1] If somebody places a baby inside, a buzzer sounds. Then a staff member comes for the baby and carries it into the home to be put into **quarantine**[2] and admitted into care. Although child abandonment is a crime in China, in this case nothing is done to **intervene**.[3]

According to China Network TV on December 21, 2013, the Shijiazhuang facility was used 183 times in two years, resulting in a much lower death rate than for babies abandoned around town. Since the overall figures for abandonment have hardly changed, the Ministry of Civil Affairs is impressed and calling for more use nationwide.

But when the City Welfare Center in Guangzhou set up a similar system in late January 2014, something went wrong. In the first two weeks 79 babies were left, and by March 16 the use of the facility had to be suspended after the number reached 262. The Center, which was equipped for 1,000 children, was caring for 1,121 and did not have beds or staff to cope with more. What probably happened is that the **publicity**[4] for the system attracted attention just before the Chinese New Year holiday, and then the news of its high rate of use set off a rush. The director of the Center explained: "Parents bring their ill babies to big cities in the hope of having them cured. But many just end up abandoning them."

The use of two English names for the drop-off facility is **intriguing**[5] because it shows two competing psychologies at work. The official name, "island of safety," is similar to the American term "safe haven" for a **designated**[6] place where a child can be given up **anonymously**[7] up to 72 hours after birth. This system began in Texas in 1999. It is illegal to abandon a baby, but at designated places, usually hospitals, the law is not enforced in this short window of time, and the name of the person bringing the child is not asked, provided the person otherwise cooperates in the interests of the child.

Chapter 11   Islands of Safety — or Baby Hatches?

The crucial difference from China is that the person does not walk away. A dialog must take place. Information about the child — except parentage — is thus obtained, and the parent's intentions can also be verified. This is especially important if the person bringing the child is not the mother. Naturally, as the system is not limited to one institution, it becomes easier to avoid the Guangzhou situation of 262 babies arriving in a surge.

The much less idealistic media name "baby hatch" comes ultimately from the "foundling wheels" set up on European orphanage walls since around 1200. The wheel was a rotating circular shelf that ran inside the orphanage wall through a hatch. The abandoner could then ring a bell and hurry away. This practice virtually disappeared in the 19th century. But variations of it have been revived recently. The best known is the "Babyklappe" installed in Hamburg, Germany since 2000. "Baby hatch" is the English translation of this name. Many European countries now use this incubator box system on a small scale, mainly outside hospitals. But it is also found outside orphanages in countries such as Pakistan, India and South Africa. The new system in China is similar.

That is to say, the incubator and blankets are similar. However, more can certainly be done to encourage communication. An information or advice letter could be left for the person bringing the baby. Or the person might be given the chance to leave a message or to request an anonymous consultation. In the German case, an eight-week reconsidering time is allowed before a court decides on any permanent arrangements for the child's future. In Hamburg, where 42 babies were left in the hatch in the ten years up to 2013, 17 of the parents contacted the hospital in this eight-week period, and 14 decided to take back the child.

In Japan, there is one facility of this kind, which has been operating since 2007 at the Jikei Hospital in Kumamoto. It has two names similar to the ones above: "baby post" (*akachan post*) to describe how it works physically, and "stork's cradle" (*konotori no yurikago*) to express the emotional side. A **commemorative**[8] TV drama about it was broadcast on the TBS channel on November 25, 2013, using the "Stork's Cradle" title.

NOTES

Guangzhou, Guangdong Province 「広東省広州市」 **Shijiazhuang, Hebei Province** 「河北省石家荘市」 **the Ministry of Civil Affairs** 「(中国の)民政部」日本の厚生労働省に相当する。 **the Chinese New Year** 「春節」中国で旧暦の正月 **Babyklappe** 「赤ちゃんポスト」ドイツのハンブルクに設置された乳幼児預り施設 **the Jikei Hospital in Kumamoto** 「熊本市にある慈恵病院」

TRUE / FALSE

Mark these statements true (T) or false (F).

1. In this system, a photo is taken when the baby is put in the incubator. [T / F]

2. The rate of use for the shelter outside the City Welfare Center in Guangzhou was as expected. [T / F]

3. The name "island of safety" reminds the writer of a "safe haven" system in the U.S.A. for people who want to abandon their babies into care. [T / F]

4. In the American system, the person bringing the child is not asked for any information about the baby. [T / F]

5. The name "baby hatch" was originally a translation from German. [T / F]

6. The German system allows an eight-week reconsidering time, but in fact very few parents return to take their baby back. [T / F]

COMPREHENSION

Answer the questions in English.

1. Why is the Chinese Ministry of Civil Affairs calling for more use of baby hatches?

2. How did the timing of the new "island of safety" facility in Guangzhou probably affect the number of babies left?

3. Which English name do you prefer for this sort of facility, "island of safety" or "baby hatch"? Why do you prefer the name?

Chapter 11 Islands of Safety – or Baby Hatches?

4. What is the difference in location between most facilities of this sort in Europe and similar facilities in Pakistan, India and South Africa?

   _____

5. How is communication encouraged in Germany between the clinic and the person bringing the baby?

   _____

GUIDED SUMMARY

Fill in the blanks with the words listed below.

The name "baby hatch" goes back to the year 2000 in Hamburg, but the idea is older and exists worldwide. In Europe, by around 1200, orphanages were being opened, and (1_____) called "foundling wheels" were set up at their doors as a way of (2_____) babies to be abandoned secretly with less danger than out of doors. Today, shelters and (3_____) may be used, but the system remains (4_____). A difficult question is how to allow (5_____) to take place between the child abandoner and the receiving institution without going against the fundamental principle that the abandoner stays (6_____).

> incubators   allowing   anonymous   similar   facilities   communication

COLUMN

　このような施設を作るには、賛否両論がありました。熊本市の慈恵病院で「赤ちゃんポスト」が開設されたのは2007年ですが、反対する理由としては「このような施設を作るというのは、無責任に赤ちゃんを託すことを奨励しているようなものだ」という意見が代表的でした。このような懸念もある中で、「一人で悩んでいる母親のために」という病院側の意向で運用が始まりました。

　「このような施設を作ると、親が育児を放棄するのを奨励するようなものだ」という反対論について個人的に、これは親に一方的に育児の責任を押しつける視野の狭い考え方のように思います。

Pirating and Streaming: Paying our Share for Media Entertainment

CHAPTER 12

インターネット技術の発展に伴って、音楽を聴く形態にも大きな変化が起きています。インターネットで音声をダウンロードする際にも、海賊版の違法な複製が増えてきています。当初はファイル互換ソフトとして広まりますが、1人がアップロードした違法コピーが次々と拡散していきます。当然、音楽業界は大打撃を受けます。

記録媒体は目まぐるしく進化します

VOCABULARY

Match these expressions from the text with the items closest in meaning in the box below.

(1) laborious ___ (2) prosecute ___ (3) alienate ___ (4) protocol ___
(5) swarm ___ (6) be entitled to ___ (7) level out ___ (8) fraction ___

a. a gathered group (of bees, etc.)	b. a small part of a whole	c. program code
d. make an enemy of	e. requiring a lot of work	f. stop falling
g. have the right to	h. take legal action against	

Chapter 12 Pirating and Streaming: Paying our Share for Media

READING

In the early 1990s, the phrase "music streaming from the speakers" might have been an annoyed person's description of a loud party. But soon afterward, "audio streaming" or "video streaming" had the more technical meaning of a continuous delivery of sound or film through a device such as a TV or a computer to a listener or viewer. The difference between this and records, audio cassettes, CDs, videos, DVDs and so on was that there was no physical package to carry away or take copies from.

Previously, streamed modes like radio and TV had been more distinct from physical ones like CDs and videos. Naturally, people could make home copies, but that was **laborious**[1] and brought a loss in quality. The copyright holders made moral appeals against "pirate copying," but their profits were still high and it hardly threatened their existence.

Things changed with the arrival of peer-to-peer file sharing ("p2p"), especially the American Napster site in 1999. Using Napster, people could post files for others to download. Millions of people took advantage of this for illegal music copying. The music recording industry **prosecuted**[2] Napster and forced it into bankruptcy in 2001. But in the process they **alienated**[3] some of their best customers because many Napster users had also been CD buyers. In any case, other sharing sites kept springing up, and soon there was no stopping them.

2001 saw the arrival of BitTorrent, a new sharing **protocol**[4] that did not require a server site or source files. Anybody could "seed" a file simply by posting up the assembly instructions. Users attracted to a seed worked together as a "**swarm**"[5] to divide the work into basic parts, which they assembled and shared. The chance of any one user being caught was small. In January to June 2012, 97 million albums were illegally copied in the U.S.A. using BitTorrent, compared with 57 million digital albums legally downloaded. Not surprisingly, behavior like this threw the recording business into a crisis. Sales of CDs and other physical music fell from $14.6 billion in 1999 to $6.3 billion by 2009. Since then, the decline has slowed but not stopped.

A new digital business model was called for, and a promising candidate in 2002 was the Open Music Model by Shuman Ghosemajumder. Ghosemajumder considered the overall contributions and rights of producers, distributors and consumers of music, and summed them up in five principles:

1. Open file sharing: Sharing is legitimate.
2. Open file formats: No restricted digital management rights.
3. Open membership: All copyright holders **are entitled to**[6] register.
4. Open payment: No controls over forms of payment.
5. Open competition: Distribution systems should develop freely.

Under conditions like these, a charge of $5 per consumer per month for unlimited downloading should be enough to ensure no loss of income for music copyright holders while removing most of the motives that encourage pirate copying.

CD2-8

Business has at least partly moved in this direction. The world's largest music distributor, iTunes Store, is now a digital-only concern, delivering music for various prices per track. A part of this money returns to the copyright holders and, since 2005, digital sales are also included in the music charts, where they influence future buying behavior. The digital market accounted for 59 percent of U.S. music sales by 2012, and this is clearly the world trend. Digital sales in the U.K. similarly reached 50 percent in 2013. In both countries, the long fall in total music sales seems at last to be **leveling out**.[7]

Not everything follows the recommendations of the Open Music Model, though. Most obviously, while iTunes Store users are encouraged to arrange their music holdings on playlists for recall, they cannot freely share them with others. In a different medium, the free online radio service Pandora goes a little further in the direction of sharing by accurately customizing the streamed music to fit the listener's preferences. The revenue comes from advertising in this case, or else from a $36 premium paid by listeners who prefer to cut out the ads.

But the major music server that probably comes closest to offering free music on demand is the Swedish site Spotify. Like Pandora, Spotify provides streamed music supported by ads, but unlike Pandora, it offers tunes, albums or artists on demand up to a limit of five plays per track. Again, users can pay to have this restriction lifted and the ads removed. Spotify pays back 70 percent of its earnings to artists and copyright holders, and says that since its launch in 2008 it has helped to reduce pirate copying in Scandinavia to a **fraction**[8] of what it was. Some artists, however, say that the rate fixed for the royalties is

Chapter 12 Pirating and Streaming: Paying our Share for Media

so small that they receive "only pennies" from all this openness.

NOTES

peer to peer「ピア・ツー・ピア」ネットワーク上で対等な関係にある端末間を相互に直接接続し、データを 送受信する通信方式。p2pと略記される。　**Napster**　音楽の共有を主目的としたファイル共有サービス　**BitTorrent**「ビットトレント」ピア・ツー・ピアを用いたファイル転送用技術

TRUE / FALSE

Mark these statements true (T) or false (F).

1. In the 1990s, "streaming" began to change its meaning from non-stop play to the continuous delivery of entertainment. [T / F]

2. In those days, profits in the music recording industry were still so high that sellers didn't worry about pirate copying too much. [T / F]

3. Napster was illegal, even when it was not used for posting pirate copies. [T / F]

4. With BitTorrent, it became possible to send file contents broken into "bits," which swarms of other users then put together again. [T / F]

5. In the U.S.A. and the U.K., more than half of music sales are digital now. [T / F]

6. Spotify's system of paying back money to artists has at last satisfied all producers and consumers of music. [T / F]

COMPREHENSION

Answer the questions in English.

1. What was the clearest distinction between "streamed" and "physical" entertainment media up until the late 1990s?

   _____

2. How did illegal downloads of albums in the U.S.A., using BitTorrent, compare with legally paid downloads in the first half of 2012?

   _____

3. Would you be willing to pay US$5 each month for unlimited downloads? Why or why not?

   _____

4. Is the fall in total music sales in the U.S.A. and the U.K. still continuing?

_____

5. In what two ways does Pandora earn its money?

_____

GUIDED SUMMARY CD2-9

Fill in the blanks with the words listed below.

After 1999, there was a long (1_____) in U.S. music sales due to the arrival of (2_____) file sharing systems, which made pirate copying easy. The downward (3_____) also occurred in other countries. The music industry needed to reorganize, and in 2002, Shuman Ghosemajumder proposed an Open Music Model, taking account of the contributions and (4_____) of producers, distributers and consumers. But in practice, the market was taken over by download companies like iTunes, who helped customers to create their own playlists, and (5_____) streaming services like Pandora and Spotify, who supplied music individually for each listener and took their income either from (6_____) or direct from the listener.

| peer-to-peer | customized | rights | trend | advertising | decline |

COLUMN

　コンパクトディスクが日本に初めてお目見えしたのは、1982年でした。それまでは直径30センチという大きさのLP(ロングプレイ)アナログディスクの市場でした。それからわずか5年でアナログディスクとコンパクトディスクの立場が逆転しました。

　コンパクトディスクが直径12センチと決められたのには、次のような経緯があります。ベートーベンの交響曲第九番(第九)は、演奏に70分以上を要する大曲です。アナログディスクの時代には30センチLP1枚に収めるため、第三楽章の途中で表裏を入れ替える必要がありました。コンパクトディスクでは片面で第九を収めるために70分以上の収録時間を確保する必要があり、それに応じて大きさが決まったということです。

Print-out Pistols: How Far should Freedoms Go?

CHAPTER 13

　3次元（3-D）印刷は、次世代の高度技術として世界の耳目を集めています。日本が得意な金型生産のように、多品種少量生産に適した技術です。しかし拳銃を作ることができるような情報がインターネット上で公開されるとなると、問題は一変します。米国テキサス州で、実際にそのような事例が発生しました。

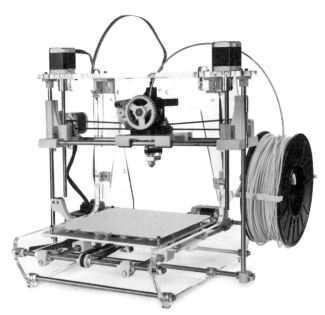

3次元印刷機

VOCABULARY

Match these expressions from the text with the items closest in meaning in the box below.

(1) sit up with a start ___ (2) presumably ___ (3) swap ___ (4) scary ___
(5) deliberate ___ (6) fundraising ___ (7) setback ___ (8) pirated ___

a. intentional b. shared without permission c. collecting money for a project d. show sudden surprise e. most likely f. exchange g. frightening h. difficulty	

READING

On May 4, 2013, a shot fired from a plastic pistol in Austin, Texas made the world **sit up with a start**.[1] It was a primitive sort of gun, holding only one bullet, and with an accuracy of aim that dropped sharply after a few shots. But what caused the alarm was that it carried no price tag and no sales controls. For a few days it was available online for nothing, so that anyone with the right sort of 3-D (three-dimensional) printer could print it out for free using the downloaded file and instructions, and then **presumably**[2] go out and shoot someone.

In retrospect, as commentators agreed, the surprise ought to have been that nobody had circulated gun recipes this way before. In particular, since the firing pin — the only metal part — is just an innocent-looking rod, this pistol makes a promising hijack weapon, whose parts can be carried onto a plane in cabin baggage with a fair chance of being missed by X-ray scans and metal detectors.

There is nothing mysterious about 3-D printing, either. Most people may remember making a landscape model by tracing height contours from a map onto cardboard and cutting out one layer for each contour level: 50 meters, 100 meters, 150 meters and so on. By gluing these cardboard layers together, a 3-D model can then be created. Since the late 1970s, the method has been automatized, coupled with digital data processing, and used in computer-aided design (CAD). In this new version, scans of an original object, or data from a virtual model designed on a screen, are used as input for printing programs.

3-D scanning uses image elements similar to the picture elements (pixels) on 2-D computer screens. On a typical screen there might be 640x480 (307,200) pixels, each of which can be used to carry visual information. In a 3-D scan, an array like this would make just one layer of the model, and several hundred other layers would be added on top, giving more than a hundred million elements. In the simplest version, each tiny element can be given a value of either one (add modeling material) or zero (do not add material). But in fact, it is usual to add more information about density, color and so on, just as in pixel imaging.

For printing, the simplest method would be to print out flat layers of material.

Chapter 13 Print-out Pistols: How Far should Freedoms Go?

But now, powders and sprays that harden into plastic are more common. Printing used to be expensive, and the first customers for the machines were manufacturing companies. But now that the material can be shot out cheaply and accurately in tiny jets, just as in ink-jet computer printing, the prices of printers are falling and some are being bought by individuals. On the Internet, you can already find sites where people **swap**[3] ideas about 3-D print modeling. Some of them are a little **scary**.[4] For example, there are people who print miniature drone aircraft as a hobby.

CD2-12

This is the background against which the print-your-own pistol became available online. In this case, it did not happen among a group of people sharing a hobby, but was a **deliberate**[5] action undertaken by a law student called Cody Wilson at the University of Texas to test whether the sharing of information for gun printing is legal under U.S. law. He wanted it to be, which was why he called his gun the "Liberator." Wilson had obtained a gun owning and manufacturing license, so that it would not have been a problem for him to make a gun at home for his own use. But the question was whether he could share his information with other people, and especially whether he could upload the complete manufacturing program on the Internet for anyone to have access to.

Wilson made no secret of his plans. He registered a campaign website, "Defense Distributed" in June, 2012, and set about **fundraising**.[6] He ran into problems on the way. The fundraising site Indiegogo dropped his campaign and the 3-D printer producer Stratasys refused to lease him a machine. But these **setbacks**[7] also brought him publicity and alternative funding support, and by May he had finished and uploaded his program. The U.S. State Department asked him to remove it again while they worked out whether it was breaking the law, and Wilson obeyed. But more advanced **pirated**[8] copies remained available on other sites. By November 2013, a more advanced printing program appeared online for a metal pistol capable of firing 50 shots.

At the moment, the risks from these weapons are small. Criminals and terrorists can find better weapons elsewhere. But as a sign of what may be expected in the future, the Liberator demands cool and careful thought. While this book was in preparation, in May 2014, the first arrest was made in Japan of a man charged with printing and owning two plastic pistols.

NOTES

Austin「オースティン」米テキサス州の州都　**firing pin**「撃針」　**pixel**　「ピクセル，画素」コンピューター・ディスプレーなどのデジタル画像を構成する最小単位　**drone aircraft**　「無人飛行機」　**print-your-own pistol**　3次元印刷による自家製の拳銃　**Indiegogo**　「インディゴーゴー」インターネット上で資金集めを行うサイトの1つ　**Stratasys**「ストラタシス社」世界で最大手の3次元印刷機製造会社　**the U.S. State Department**「米国務省」

TRUE / FALSE

Mark these statements true (T) or false (F).

1. This plastic pistol went on firing accurately time after time. [T / F]

2. It was in 2013 that gun recipes were first circulated on the Internet. [T / F]

3. 3-D printing is a layer-by-layer modeling process controlled by a digital program. [T / F]

4. It will still be some time before 3-D printers come down in price enough to be bought by individuals. [T / F]

5. It was clear from the start that Cody Wilson had broken the law. [T / F]

6. At the moment, the threat from 3-D pistols is relatively small because criminals and terrorists can find better weapons elsewhere. [T / F]

COMPREHENSION

Answer the questions in English.

1. Why does a pistol like this make a promising hijack weapon?

2. What sorts of things can be used as input for 3-D models?

3. Why did Cody Wilson call his gun the "Liberator"?

4. How did Cody Wilson try to collect money for his gun-making project at first?

Chapter 13 Print-out Pistols: How Far should Freedoms Go?

5. What sort of person would be attracted to 3-D gun printing in Japan, do you think?

___

GUIDED SUMMARY   CD2-13

Fill in the blanks with the words listed below.

3-D printers were once expensive machines used in (1_____) companies or engineering labs to produce models of objects created on screen using a design software. But they now use an ink-jet (2_____) similar to the kind used in computer printers, which enables them to print models more (3_____) and cheaply. With this, the 3-D printer is turning into a hobby tool. The problem is that, with the (4_____) of a 3-D scanner or of data downloaded from the Internet, it will soon be (5_____) of printing anything, (6_____) or illegal, including much more dangerous versions of Cody Wilson's "Liberator" pistol.

legal   manufacturing   aid   capable   accurately   technology

COLUMN

　次世代の技術と呼び声の高い3次元プリンター技術、利用の仕方によっては、両刃の剣になりかねません。本文で紹介したような拳銃製造は、「百害あって一利なし」でしょう。それでもこれをインターネット上で公開しようというのは、いかにも米国らしい考え方だと思えます。良い方への利用としては、臓器模型作成などが挙げられそうです。心臓などの臓器を3次元で複製することによって、手術の予行演習をするという利用方法が確立されているそうです。

　金型というのは大量生産をする場合に欠かせない技術で、日本が得意としていた分野でした。金型の見本を制作する際にも、3次元プリンターの技術が活躍する場面が目前に迫っているように思われます。

Smart Reality: Computer Games Return to the Physical World

CHAPTER 14

　1980年代に家庭用ゲーム機が発売されて以来、テレビゲームは日本のお家芸でした。今はまた「密室脱出ゲーム」という分野で世界を牽引しているようです。このゲームは仮想現実から実際の密室脱出へと、逆の経路を辿ったという点でも注目に値しそうです。

密室脱出ゲームが入居している建物の外観

VOCABULARY

Match these expressions from the text with the items closest in meaning in the box below.

(1) furnishings ___   (2) pixel ___   (3) collaborate ___   (4) penetrate ___
(5) coincidence ___   (6) torture ___   (7) intuitive ___   (8) fume ___

a. feel impatient	b. furniture and other fittings	c. work together
d. feeling-based rather than logical	e. chance similarity	f. go inside
g. smallest-size picture element	h. deliberate causing of pain	

Chapter 14 Smart Reality: Computer Games Return to the Physical World

READING

If you are into electronic gaming, you may have noticed the recent rise of a genre called Room Escape, in which someone in a closed room has to find a way to escape based on information and objects concealed in the **furnishings**.[1] The idea was developed in Kyoto around 2004 by people connected with the *SCRAP* game magazine, and spread around Japan and East Asia. In 2007, the same people then created a version using real-life rooms. However, worldwide interest was not attracted until 2012, when the Californian branch of *SCRAP* put on a similar event called *Escape from the Mysterious Room*, followed up quickly by *Escape from the Haunted Ship* and *Escape from the Time Travel Lab*.

To show the gist, here is the starting scenario for *Escape from the Mysterious Room*:

You awaken, and find yourself locked inside a room.
It has a desk, chairs, a carpet – everything seems normal.
But on closer inspection you find a series of mysterious codes …
There are ten others in the room with you.
Will you be able to escape?

There are two points to notice here. It is clearly necessary to inspect the room. But it is also relevant that "there are ten others" with you. It takes coordinated play to escape. The room's secrets have to be used together and in a particular order, and there may be places in the action where one task cannot be performed until something else has been done to prepare for it. In some cases, this support task can only be supplied by another person.

The relationship between electronic and real Room Escape games is interesting to trace. In electronic Room Escape, you beam a cursor around the room and receive signals when it locates hidden keys, cards, tools, etc. When you have enough of these, you can begin using them, in sets or in combination with other information, to explore further. Sometimes you can also unlock secrets by solving puzzles or rearranging the room fittings. As new information emerges, you gradually gain access to more game space. But in some places, as has been said, you will be blocked and thrown back on the support of your fellow players.

The earliest video games in this genre were released in the 1980s, when **pixel**[2] techniques advanced far enough to allow objects to be invisibly concealed in a larger screen picture. Three early examples were *Maniac Mansion* (1987), with
5 a scenario of teenagers rescuing someone from a horror house, *The Secret of Monkey Island* (1990), based on themes from the *Pirates of the Caribbean* ride at Disneyland, and *Day of the Tentacle* (1993), in which characters in different periods of history **collaborate**[3] across time to stop a creature from taking over the world. In all of these, characters equipped with different strengths and
10 weaknesses work together to **penetrate**[4] the domain of an enemy, search for clues, and perform a rescue. It cannot be a **coincidence**[5] that the *SCRAP* Real Escape games in California also have these scenarios of a mysterious interior, a haunted ship and a time travel lab.　　　　　　　　　　　　CD2-16

The Californian *SCRAP* events represent the commercial entertainment face
15 of Real Escape. Most other escape rooms are smaller startups, with names such as *Live Escape Game, Adventure Rooms, ParaParks, HintQuest, ClueQuest* and *HintHunt*. The type of room used varies from plain-looking apartments or offices to **torture**[6] chambers or zombie dens, and real location games are also staged, especially in Asia, in places such as schools, hospitals and amusement parks.
20 The nature of the hints also varies, with more emphasis on reasoning in some escape rooms and more faith in **intuitive**[7] observation in others. Some room operators feed in hints to teams who get stuck; others leave them to **fume**.[8]

Two almost universal features are that Real Escape is a team challenge, not an individual one, and that one session lasts 60 minutes. There are reasons for
25 this. For one thing, the room gets disarranged in the course of a session and resetting it for one player is not economical. For another, a 60-minute session is found to give players just the right pitch of involvement, while allowing the room to be used six or seven times a day.

Going back to the grand-daddy of escape games *Maniac Mansion*, one
30 enriching feature in it was that the hero, Dave, goes into the horror house with two other "kids" out of a group of six. Each kid has different capabilities, and depending on what happens inside, the choice of kids will affect the chance of getting out alive. Few scientific studies of escape room strategy probably exist yet. But surely a mixed team ought to do better than a uniform one. It seems

Chapter 14 Smart Reality: Computer Games Return to the Physical World

that some users of these rooms are corporations who send in groups of staff as an exercise in professional teamwork.

NOTES

SCRAP 密室脱出ゲームなどを企画運営する会社（元は、ゲーム雑誌の題）　*Live Escape Game* スイスのチューリヒにある密室脱出ゲーム　*Adventure Rooms* 米コネティカット州にある密室脱出ゲーム　*ParaParks* ハンガリーのブダペストにある密室脱出ゲーム　*HintQuest* ドイツのミュンヘンにある密室脱出ゲーム　*ClueQuest, HintHunt* ともにロンドンにある密室脱出ゲーム

TRUE / FALSE

Mark these statements true (T) or false (F).

1. A new genre of games called Room Escape has become increasingly popular since 2004. [T / F]

2. In *Escape from the Mysterious Room*, all that is needed in order to escape is a close inspection of the room's furnishings. [T / F]

3. In many Room Escape games, keys, cards, tools, and so on can only be used after you have collected a certain number or combination of them. [T / F]

4. The *SCRAP* games in California were created completely independently from the earlier video escape games of the 1980s. [T / F]

5. Sixty minutes is too long for a Real Escape game session. [T / F]

6. The outcome of the game changes in *Maniac Mansion*, depending on which other kids Dave chooses to go into the house with. [T / F]

COMPREHENSION

Answer the questions in English.

1. What are the special characteristics of the Room Escape game genre?

   _____

2. What are two points to notice in the starting scenario for *Escape from the Mysterious Room*?

   _____

3. In what way did the development of the first video escape games depend on advances in pixel techniques?

   _____

69

4. What kinds of places are chosen for real location escape games in Asia and elsewhere?

   _____

5. Which sort of team would do better in a Real Escape session, a team of members who behave similarly, or a team with a greater mix of members?

   _____

GUIDED SUMMARY

Fill in the blanks with the words listed below.

Room Escape is a game genre that ($_1$ _____) in electronic games, and later evolved into a version using ($_2$ _____) rooms. Players first prepare for the game by reading the ($_3$ _____). Then they begin their explorations, which usually also involve ($_4$ _____). The electronic and real room versions have a good deal ($_5$ _____). For example, they both involve searches for objects such as keys, cards, or tools, which can then be used to open up more game space. There are also some differences, however. For one thing, in Real Room Escape a time limit is usually set. The most common limit for one ($_6$ _____) is 60 minutes.

---

scenario   in common   real-life   originated   session   teamwork

---

COLUMN

　現実版脱出ゲームは2007年、京都で開業しました。それ以来、全国に常設の施設ができました。また遊園地などが期間限定で開設することもあります。数人一組で謎を解きながら密室から抜け出すという遊びは、知恵を出し合って意思疎通を図るという「副産物」効果もあります。この効果を当て込んで、新入社員の研修や婚活に使おうという動きも全国で見られます。また自治体が加わって「町興し」に役立てるという例も出てきました。沖縄県宮古島市で開催されたゲームでは10日間で約3,000人を集めました。

　家庭用ゲーム機の登場以来ずっと日本のお家芸だったゲームの世界に、「脱出ゲーム」という新しい分野が花開いたのかもしれません。

Seven Days, Six Nights and a Run: A Special Interest Tour

CHAPTER 15

　毎年 11 月第 1 日曜に開催されるニューヨークシティー・マラソン。5 万人の出走者のうち、日本の旅行会社が 600 人の枠を持っています。航空運賃と宿泊料はツアー料金に含まれますが、マラソン参加料や空港・ホテル間の往復交通費は参加者の負担です。世界各地の大都市で市民参加のマラソンは増えていますが、人気が高まって出場するのは年々難しくなる一方のようです。旅行会社も、あの手この手で集客の工夫をしています。

ニューヨークのタイムズ広場

VOCABULARY

Match these expressions from the text with the items closest in meaning in the box below.

(1) hassle ___　(2) a second string ___　(3) fall back on ___　(4) subsidiary ___
(5) courier ___　(6) precaution ___　(7) sendoff ___　(8) staid ___

a. try using instead	b. annoyance	c. serious and conservative	d. farewell
e. small company operated by a larger one		f. security measure	
g. another plan in reserve		h. travel or tour assistant	

While fewer people are attracted to mass tours nowadays, there is still a demand for activity trips for participants who share special interests: wine tours, archeology tours, trekking, diving, cooking trips and the like. The attraction of a tour of this sort will be greatest if it saves the customer the trouble of making separate arrangements for the travel and accommodation, and above all for the activity program.

A good example of how a special interest tour can make complex arrangements simple is a trip from Japan for people hoping to run in the New York City Marathon on the first Sunday in November. Naturally, it is possible to apply to enter individually through the official website and have your name put into the draw for running places held in late March. The official website explains the procedure, and later, if your name is drawn, provides further advice for race preparations. But none of this is very simple unless you are used to it, and to remove the various complications, a cash-down deal of "Seven days, six nights and a run" with no extra **hassle**[1] might be tempting. As it happens, the New York City Marathon has five official Travel Partners in Japan — four of them mainstream travel agents — who advertise offers of this sort. But the customer cannot pick and choose. Taking part in the race is offered as part of a package, along with the flight and hotel reservations.

Another attraction in entering the marathon this way is that it brings an advantage denied to individual applicants unless they qualify as "elite athletes": a guaranteed running place. A further group of customers for this sort of tour, therefore, are individual applicants eliminated in the March draw, who regard the package arrangement as **a second string**[2] to **fall back on**.[3] In fact, even some runners who survive the draw seem to appreciate the convenience of a guaranteed hotel room near to the finish line. The Travel Partners try to attract them with small discounts from the regular tour price.

If you run in the New York City Marathon using a special offer like this, how much does it cost and how much support for the race can you expect? Looking at one of the Travel Partner sites, run by the U.S. **subsidiary**[4] of a large Japanese travel group, the basic offer for 2013, using economy-class flights, was a package of between five and seven days, departing on October 31 or November 1 for a November 3 race. The price ranged between ¥226,000 with

Chapter 15   Seven Days, Six Nights and a Run: A Special Interest Tour

three hotel stays and ¥282,000 with five, using a hotel on Central Park. This was for a shared room, with the option of a single for ¥30,000 per night extra. This part of the package was definitely not cheap, but a special premium may have been in force for the marathon week.

Support for the runner was limited in this case. A company **courier**[5] was on hand to solve problems, and on the morning of the race, group transit was provided to the starting line, with the additional encouragement of a "bento" breakfast to eat on the way. But no other meals were included, and there was no transit organized from and to the airport. Collecting the race name card was also the runner's responsibility, but that may have been an ID **precaution**[6] on the part of the marathon organizers. The payment of the fee for entering the race was up to the runner, too. All in all, this was a basics-only kind of trip, although in a nice hotel, for people whose chief concern on arriving would have been their pre-race training in Central Park.

CD2-20

Although this trip was advertised as a marathon tour, there is not much in the arrangements that is specific to running. The company's courier may have had a few running tips to share, but apart from that, the same pattern of support would have worked as well for a group interested in seeing Broadway musicals. What attracts customers more is the fact that the New York City Marathon sets aside 600 guaranteed running places (out of 50,000) for its Japanese Travel Partners, who then have little trouble in selling them on further in package deals.

On the Internet there are also smaller tour operators who concentrate more systematically on special interests. The basic travel and stay arrangements may be roughly the same as above: economy class, no transits, room sharing. But more attention is paid to promoting a group spirit among the participants. The tour leaders are people with running backgrounds, who supply racing advice, show participants around parts of the course, or lead training activities for those who want them. They may also meet participants at the finish, or hold a **sendoff**[7] party at the end. Naturally, this is part of a sound business strategy: the same operator will be offering tours for similar events around the world and the best customers are repeat ones.

Smaller specialist operators of this sort tend to have company names ending in "… club." It isn't easy to tell how genuinely independent they are from the larger tour companies, however. Indeed, the suspicion arises that they might even be the fun subsidiaries of the same operators who put more **staid**[8] runners, two-to-a-room, in the hotels closer to the finish line.

NOTES

Central Park「セントラルパーク」マンハッタン島中央に位置する東西800メートル、南北約4.5キロの公園　**basics-only**　食事なしで飛行機便と宿泊のみというように、必要最小限だけを備えた旅行の類い。　**Broadway**「ブロードウェイ」ニューヨーク市のマンハッタン島南半分を南北に貫く通り。43丁目から55丁目にかけてミュージカル劇場が集中している。

TRUE / FALSE

Mark these statements true (T) or false (F).

1. You cannot apply directly from Japan to run in the New York City Marathon. [T / F]

2. The procedures and preparations explained on the marathon website are simple to follow from Japan, even for first-timers. [T / F]

3. Some people already assured of a running place still sign up for the package tour as a way of getting a hotel room near to the finish line. [T / F]

4. On the morning of the race, the tour participants have to make their own way to the starting point. [T / F]

5. The participants have to go up in person to pay the race entry fee. [T / F]

6. The marathon organizers set aside just over one percent of running places to be sold in package deals in Japan. [T / F]

COMPREHENSION

Answer the questions in English.

1. What is the greatest convenience of a special interest tour?

2. How might a marathon package tour help people in Japan who try for a non-guaranteed running place in the March draw but are unlucky?

3. Do you think that a package price of ¥226,000 for a run, a round-trip flight and a three-night hotel stay is reasonable? What price would you have expected?

Chapter 15 Seven Days, Six Nights and a Run: A Special Interest Tour

4. What other support services do more specialized marathon tour operators offer runners?

   _____

5. Do the authors feel that the smaller, more specialized operators are totally independent from the large tour companies?

   _____

GUIDED SUMMARY
CD2-21

Fill in the blanks with the words listed below.

The New York City Marathon is held on the first Sunday in (1_____). If you want to apply for a non-guaranteed running place, you can put your name in for the draw, in late (2_____). But if you live in Japan and find this procedure a (3_____), you may prefer a package deal offering the trip and the run together. This is an example of a "special interest tour." In the most basic case, in addition to an (4_____) running place, the package might cover flights and hotel stays but no meals. Marathon tours are (5_____) by four large Japanese travel firms, using an allowance of 600 guaranteed running places set aside by the race organizers. Some of the business is also passed on to smaller, specialist operators, who offer more in the way of positive (6_____) and encouragement.

| March | November | assured | support | hassle | operated |

COLUMN

　ニューヨーク市はスタテン島、ブルックリン、ブロンクス、クィーンズ、マンハッタンの5区(Borough)に分けられています。ニューヨークシティー・マラソンでは、この5区全てを走るようにコースが設定されています。マンハッタン島だけでも南北15キロ以上という細長い地形ですから、ゴールから近いホテルに泊まるというのは旅行会社にとっては売り込みの材料になりそうです。

　東京マラソンは2013年大会から、世界6大都市マラソンの1つとなりました。ロンドン、ボストン、ベルリン、シカゴ、ニューヨークの有名都市マラソンで構成される「ワールド・マラソン・メジャーズ(WMM)」に東京マラソンが加わり、世界6大マラソンとなりました。

Fracking: Cracks in the Ground beneath our Feet

CHAPTER 16

近年、米国ではシェールガスが世界のエネルギー事情に「革命」を起こすとわれています。頁岩（シェール）層から採取される天然ガスや石油によって、米国がエネルギー資源の輸入国から輸出国に大転換する可能性が現実的になってきています。しかし頁岩からガスや石油を取り出すために水蒸気や化学薬品を注入するので、地下水汚染などの環境問題にも注意を払わなければなりません。

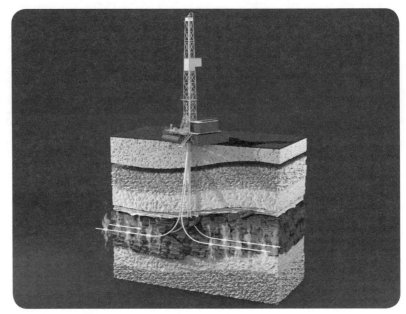

シェールガス堀削の概念図

VOCABULARY

Match these expressions from the text with the items closest in meaning in the box below.

(1) drawback ___ (2) inject ___ (3) fissure ___
(4) geothermal ___ (5) groundwater ___ (6) demonize ___
(7) concealment ___ (8) in the medium term ___

a. treat as evil	b. crack	c. disadvantage
d. for a fairly long time to come		
e. pump in	f. using underground heat	g. water available below the ground
h. hiding something		

Chapter 16 Fracking: Cracks in the Ground beneath our Feet

READING

CD2-22

For a few years after the 1973 oil crisis, people were alarmed that a peak in fossil fuel production had been reached and that energy prices would be taking a permanent upward turn. Now this seems premature. With a broader mix of energy sources, most countries' dependence on oil and gas is actually smaller. Admittedly, Japan's situation is special now, with its nuclear alternative switched off. For Japan, there is no use denying it: oil is getting scarcer.

One possible response is to take a second look at resources which were previously not worth thinking about, for example, oil and gas extracted from shale. Shale oil is a less efficient substitute for petroleum. But it can be upgraded by adding hydrogen. It was once used as a local fuel in many countries, but with petroleum available, it was reduced to a standby status in times of shortage. With the oil crisis, shale oil had a temporary comeback in the U.S.A. Then in 2005, it returned permanently. This time, there was a more strategic focus on how to lower production costs, while improving the quality and minimizing the environmental **drawbacks**.[1]

Although shale can also be mined and treated on the surface, it is cheaper to process underground. This allows more to be taken and reduces the direct damage to the environment. For both oil and gas, there are two main production steps: fracturing and extraction.

CD2-23

1. Fracturing

    The media call this "fracking." A fluid (water, steam, CO_2, etc.) is **injected**[2] into the shale, opening up **fissures**.[3] The fluid contains acids or other chemicals to weaken the rock, and usually grains of sand, which enter into the fissures and keep them open.

2. Extraction:

    To extract oil, the shale is heated with steam or CO_2 gas, or by some other method. The gas in the shale may burn too, assisting the process.

    To extract gas, more water is pumped in. The escaping gas dissolves into the water and flows up to the surface with it.

The term "shale fracking" is used emotively in the media. But rock fracturing is not used only for shale oil and gas; in America, it is also used in gas extraction generally, in mineral mining, or in the pumping up of hot water for **geothermal**[4] heating.

But this widespread use doesn't make it harmless. There are several reasons why other countries have tried to avoid this method. For one thing, even if nothing escapes into the air or is left on the surface, the underground pollution from the carbon and acids pollutes the **groundwater**.[5] Second, huge amounts of water are used, and need to be cleaned afterward. If the water is transported from a distance this will also increase fuel emissions, while if local water is used the groundwater will sink. Third, the input of energy is high compared with the amount of fuel extracted. And fourth, if rocks are fractured over a wide area, this leaves risks for the future. The fractures create strains, which go on accumulating. The first sinkholes may open up to 50 years later. CD2-24

Some of these problems exist with other fuel-extracting processes as well, and there is no special reason to **demonize**[6] shale. But the risks should be seen, and it is best that they should be seen in advance. Only then can people form a realistic idea of what is being proposed in their country or region. In Japan, the **concealments**[7] of information around Fukushima Daiichi show the importance of this.

In America, people are talking of a "Shale Revolution." The calculation behind this is that the cost of extracting shale oil and gas is coming down near to a level where it can compete with petroleum. If petroleum rises in price, shale-based fuels will be there to replace it. But that is not all. Shale oil and gas are abundant in northern regions, and North America seems to have more of them than anywhere. **In the medium term**,[8] economically, this will mean that the U.S.A. can return to being an exporter of oil. In the longer term, politically, it may also mean that America will find itself under less pressure from its various petroleum-rich partners or rivals.

Japan joined this game late, but in September 2013, Mitsui & Co. announced its entry into a project in the Eagle Ford Shale field in Texas. It will be some years before this translates into an oil supply. In the meantime, Japan will have to go on importing petroleum and gas at high prices. Modestly but historically, a firm called JAPEX carried out Japan's first "frack job" for shale oil in October 2012, obtaining 100 kl of liquid from a site in Akita. This gave 31 kl of crude oil in the immediate term. In the long-term future, who knows? A sinkhole may or may not follow.

Chapter 16 Fracking: Cracks in the Ground beneath our Feet

NOTES

the 1973 oil crisis「1973年石油危機」第四次中東戦争によりこの年、原油価格が一挙に4倍近くに高騰した。　**shale**「頁岩」　**fracturing**「破砕」　**extraction**「抽出」　**Mitsui & Co.**「三井物産」　**JAPEX** = Japan Petroleum Exploration Co., Ltd.「石油資源開発株式会社」　**sinkhole**「空洞」

TRUE / FALSE

Mark these statements true (T) or false (F).

1. There is less direct damage to the outside environment if shale is mined and treated on the surface rather than underground.　　　[T / F]

2. The same fluids are pumped in to extract both gas and oil from shale.　　　[T / F]

3. Rock fracturing is also used for regular gas extraction in the U.S.A.　　　[T / F]

4. Shale fracking is harmless in spite of the use of acids.　　　[T / F]

5. The cost of extracting shale oil and gas is steadily coming down.　　　[T / F]

6. Recently, enough shale oil is already being extracted in Japan to supply the nation's domestic demand.　　　[T / F]

COMPREHENSION

Answer the questions in English.

1. Why does it seem premature to talk of a severe shortage of fossil fuels in the immediate future, except in Japan?

2. Shale oil is not a highly efficient fuel, but how can its performance be upgraded?

3. What other substances are usually mixed in with the fracking fluid to weaken the rock and to keep the fissures open?

4. Why is it important not to conceal information about the real risks associated with energy extraction?

5. What medium-term economic benefit will the U.S.A. obtain from the Shale Revolution?

___

GUIDED SUMMARY   CD2-25

Fill in the blanks with the words listed below.

The oil and gas locked up in shale have to be (1_____). In the past, this work was performed above ground, but now underground extraction is (2_____). The shale layer is fractured by injecting a fluid such as water, steam, or (3_____), along with corroding acids. Then oil can be forced out using (4_____) (e.g., from steam), or gas can be dissolved in water and carried to the (5_____). Although the resulting damage is not visible above ground, there is a serious risk of groundwater (6_____) and of future sinkholes. There is a lot of talk of a Shale Revolution in the United States at the moment, but the environmental costs of extracting shale oil and gas must be carefully monitored.

> heat   carbon dioxide   extracted   cheaper   pollution   surface

COLUMN

　石油や石炭などの化石燃料のうち、石油は特に埋蔵されている地球上の地域に偏りがありました。「シェールガス革命」は、そのような地理的偏在を大きく変える可能性を秘めています。日本は天然資源に乏しく、東日本大震災以降に原子力発電所が停止してからは燃料の輸入によって貿易赤字が増大する一方です。

　そのような中では、日本近海に埋蔵が確認されているメタンハイドレートに期待が集まっています。メタンは炭素原子1個と水素原子4個が結合した有機物で、「ハイドレート」というのは水分子が籠状の構造で他の分子を取り込んでいる物質です。新エネルギー「メタンハイドレート」の商業化が実現すれば、日本のエネルギー事情も大きく変わるでしょう。

Two World Heritage Food Traditions: Washoku and Kimchi

CHAPTER 17

2013年12月、「和食」が無形文化遺産に登録されました。文化遺産と自然遺産の2種類は申請件数が増えて、世界遺産への登録は激戦の様相を呈してきました。新たに「無形文化遺産」という分類ができ、より多様な申請が出されるようになりました。和食の先行例で参考となったのがフランスとメキシコの料理で、申請を同時に出したのが韓国のキムジャン（キムチ作り）でした。

美しく盛り付けられた和食

VOCABULARY

Match these expressions from the text with the items closest in meaning in the box below.

(1) craftsmanship ___ (2) accompanying ___ (3) transmit ___ (4) safeguard ___
(5) gastronomy ___ (6) refinement ___ (7) affinity ___ (8) guise ___

| a. sense of closeness | b. protect | c. creative work skill | d. way, form |
| e. delicacy of development | f. hand on | g. art of serving food | h. associated |

In Chapter 3 (Mount Fuji), it was said that world heritage used to be pictured too simply in terms of *sites*. There have been moves away from this, and recently UNESCO has been listing less physical sorts of heritage, starting with a "Memory of the World" program which began preserving documents in 1997. But this still leaves countless oral and enacted traditions. To fill this gap, a Convention for the Safeguarding of the Intangible Cultural Heritage was signed in 2003 for domains such as oral traditions, performing arts, rituals and events, interactions with nature, and traditional **craftsmanship**.[1]

For this intangible cultural heritage, a "representative list" of practices is kept, on which countries apply to have outstanding traditions "inscribed." In 2013, *Washoku* became Japan's 22nd entry on this list. According to Isao Kumakura, president of Shizuoka University of Art and Culture, who led the promotion campaign, this general name *Washoku* was chosen to avoid connections with particular dishes. *Washoku* means "the traditional foods that Japanese regularly eat at home and on a daily basis," along with the practices of balancing, making and serving them, and the **accompanying**[2] manners and customs.

A representative practice must meet five criteria: First, it must be **transmitted**[3] as a part of social life. Second, it must help people fit into their social and natural surroundings. Third, measures are to be taken to **safeguard**[4] it. Fourth, the application must be prepared with broad participation from communities and groups. Fifth, the practice must already be on the country's own intangible cultural heritage inventory.

Concerning the first two criteria, the presentation supporting the application stressed that *Washoku* is common to all parts of Japan, while allowing regional differences. It favors the consumption of a varied, healthy, seasonal and generally local diet, with a focus on fish, rice, vegetables and wild plants. Preparing and sharing this food contributes to a spirit of cooperation, respect and harmony at the family, community and national levels, and alongside these constant features there are also customs for special occasions, especially New Year.

After the inscription, President Kumakura made some interview remarks which might surprise people who misunderstand World Heritage status as an award for uniqueness. Actually, he said, the decision to propose *Washoku* was inspired by the success of two earlier proposals in 2010, one for French

Chapter 17 Two World Heritage Food Traditions: Washoku and Kimchi

gastronomy,[5] and the other for rural eating in Mexico. The blending of foods and the concern for harmony in the *Washoku* presentation owe more to the French proposal, while the respect for nature and the seasons owes more to the Mexican one. The argument linking *Washoku* to New Year customs also matches an argument connecting corn cakes and the Mexican Day of the Dead festival.

Naturally, if Japanese food did not have the qualities described in the proposal presentation, it would not have been inscribed on the UNESCO list. But inscribing it is not only a mark of special status. It is also a statement of what it has in common with other food traditions. The resemblance with French gastronomy on one side and Mexican rural cooking on the other may actually be a good key for the understanding of *Washoku*. According to President Kumakura, the balance between social **refinement**[6] and **affinity**[7] to nature in it reflects an adjustment of styles in the cosmopolitan Taisho period. Before then, Japanese eating was more countrified.

Another food tradition proposed and inscribed in 2013 was "*Kimjang* — making and sharing kimchi" in the Republic of Korea. It is interesting to compare the presentation description for this with the one for *Washoku*, as well.

"Kimchi" would have been a simpler naming choice, but kimchi is strictly a product, not a practice. *Kimjang* means "kimchi pickling" and normally refers to the preparation of the winter kimchi reserve in November. It is this connection with winter that gives the tradition its meaning. The annual pickling task acts as a reminder of how people once needed to work together in families to conserve and share food resources, while supporting one another at the neighborly and national levels as well. There is something in common here with the *Washoku* presentation, which also focuses on a recurring winter event. Only the Korean story is about endurance rather than New Year renewal.

In modern South Korea, less than half of all households pickle their own winter kimchi now, but the ones that still do send stocks of it to their city-based children or relatives. In this changed **guise**,[8] *Kimjang* continues to contribute to the maintenance of family ties. As in Japan, local authorities, schools and citizen groups attempt to preserve the old ways through education and events, while a more personal experience can be to visit remote mountain villages to see kimchi prepared in the cold and then buried underground in storage pots.

NOTES

Isao Kumakura, president of Shizuoka University of Art and Culture「静岡文化芸術大学の熊倉功夫学長」 **the Day of the Dead**「死者の日」南米諸国で11月1日と2日に行われる故人を追憶する祝祭。特にメキシコで盛大に行われる。 **the cosmopolitan Taisho period**「コスモポリタンな大正時代」政党内閣や洋装など、第1次世界大戦と日中戦争の戦間期で比較的自由な大正時代をいう。 **countrified**「田舎風の」

TRUE / FALSE

Mark these statements true (T) or false (F).

1. *Washoku* was chosen as a general term to describe distinctive food traditions in Japanese life. [T / F]

2. One criterion for a representative practice is that it helps people to live in harmony with their social and natural surroundings. [T / F]

3. Despite regional differences, *Washoku* is basically similar all over Japan. [T / F]

4. The Day of the Dead is a traditional Mexican New Year festival. [T / F]

5. The *Washoku* tradition we know today goes back to the early 19th century. [T / F]

6. *Kimjang* is the name of a food product, not a traditional practice. [T / F]

COMPREHENSION

Answer the questions in English.

1. What kinds of heritage are preserved in the Memory of the World project?

2. Why was the term *Washoku* more suitable than just "Japanese foods"?

3. What two proposals in 2010 inspired President Kumakura's team to campaign for the inscription of *Washoku* on the representative list?

4. At what time in the year do Korean people prepare their winter reserve of kimchi?

Chapter 17 Two World Heritage Food Traditions: Washoku and Kimchi

5. How does the annual custom of *Kimjang* help Koreans to maintain strong family ties?

_____

GUIDED SUMMARY   CD2-29

Fill in the blanks with the words listed below.

In addition to its cultural and natural World Heritage sites, UNESCO now also engages in other kinds of heritage (1_____), including an Intangible Cultural Heritage program for traditional oral and (2_____) practices. In 2013, Japan's distinctive food culture, *Washoku*, was (3_____) as a representative practice under this program. That is to say, it was recognized as a set of shared behaviors that help Japanese people to (4_____) into their social and natural environment. In the same year, South Korea inscribed *Kimjang*, the communal tradition of pickling kimchi as a food (5_____) for the winter. This may not be vital for survival anymore, but it remains as a symbol of (6_____) and as a reminder of the importance of maintaining strong family and neighborhood ties.

fit	conservation	inscribed	reserve	enacted	endurance

COLUMN

　世界遺産は、日本でいえば寺社仏閣など「有形」の場所を指定する制度でした。それに対して無形文化遺産は、「手で触れることができない」文化的側面や芸能などに焦点を当てているようです。日本でこれまで指定された無形文化遺産には、能楽、人形浄瑠璃、歌舞伎、雅楽などの伝統芸能や、京都の祇園祭のような行事が含まれています。

　第3の分類である「記憶遺産」には、日本から3件が登録されています。山本作兵衛炭鉱記録画・記録文書(2011年)、慶長遣欧使節関係資料(日本／スペイン共通、2013年)、御堂関白記(2013年)です。

A Restored View of Old Edo?

CHAPTER 18

　1960年代は、日本の高度経済成長の真っただ中でした。折しも1964年の五輪開催に向けて都心では高速道路を急いで造りました。用地買収を避け、最短距離で通すために、川の上に高架道路を建設しました。半世紀を経て、景観を重視する考えから高架高速道路の見直し論も出ています。江戸時代の五街道の起点となった日本橋も、頭上を高速道路が通っています。その日本橋周辺で再開発事業が進行中です。

現代の日本橋

VOCABULARY

Match these expressions from the text with the items closest in meaning in the box below.

(1) gloom ___　(2) streetscape ___　(3) provocation ___　(4) crass ___
(5) artery ___　(6) plaque ___　(7) eyesore ___　(8) persistent ___

a. view of a street	b. ugly construction	c. plate, sign	d. call of opposition
e. never ending	f. half-darkness	g. main road	h. insensitive, extreme

Chapter 18 A Restored View of Old Edo?

READING

CD2-30

  In March 2014, two new buildings with shopping and restaurant floors, cultural facilities and offices opened in the Muromachi section of Nihonbashi: the 116-meter Coredo 2 and the 80-meter Coredo 3. Together with the 105-meter Coredo Muromachi completed in 2010, they line up on the same cherry-tree-lined avenue as the Bank of Japan, the Mitsui Building and the Mitsukoshi Department Store. The Coredo buildings all share the retro feature of a stepped stonework base section 100 shaku (30 meters) high continuing the roofline of the older prewar buildings. Above this, they soar up into steel and glass upper structures as pendants to the 195-meter Mitsui Tower of 2005, which is set off to one side of the avenue. The name "Coredo" signifies that the new buildings form a unitary architectural group harmonizing with the old "core of Edo" and respecting its values even while transcending them.

  The site owners are different, but the constructor in each case was Mitsui Fudosan, and the overall designer was Norihiko Dan, a great grandson of the prewar head of the Mitsui group. There is also another Coredo building across the Nihonbashi River but still aligned with the rest: the 121-meter Coredo Nihonbashi completed in 2004. Coredo Nihonbashi and the Mitsui Tower have another 100-shaku stepped base feature in common, although in this case it does not go right round the buildings and does not try to replicate stonework.

  Interestingly, the unity of this group of buildings was already broken at the time they were built. Since 1963, it has been impossible to stand on one bank of the Nihonbashi River and look across at the other because of the way the inner circle of the Metropolitan Expressway clings just above the water on its sweep round from Edobashi to Kandabashi. The only way to see both banks at once is from a riverboat or from one of the bridges. Here, from the **gloom**[1] under the highway, it is just possible to catch glimpses of **streetscape**[2] on either side. In this sense, the line of Coredo buildings can also be seen as a **provocation**.[3] The architect seems to be appealing for the old view across the river to be reopened.

CD2-31

  This is not the only stretch of old city in Japan to have been buried under highways. But it is an especially **crass**[4] example for two reasons. First, it was done in a rush for the 1964 Olympics, when following the river was the only way of opening an **artery**[5] into the city center in time. And second, this was

87

a historically outstanding location, marking the start of land routes out of Edo after the establishment of the Tokugawa Shogunate. By the 18th century, Nihonbashi was the starting point for five great highways that branched out to different regions of Japan. There is a **plaque**[6] in the road marking the highway departure point, but today it is unapproachable to anyone except road repairers. Ordinary people can only see the nearby replica.

The building of the Coredo Nihonbashi and the Mitsui Tower coincided with an urban renewal campaign to restore the area to the sort of distinction it had when the districts between the bridge and the castle were the prime locations for the cloth, metal and other trades in the Tokugawa city. In Meiji times, there was further growth around the bridge, where the Bank of Japan and Stock Exchange still stand. The prewar presence of Mitsui and the other business groups is less visible now, however, and on one level the Coredo constructions, with their signature links to older buildings, may represent an attempt to recall this history. Environmentally, they more simply express the wish to remove **eyesores**[7] dating from the rapid growth era and find a way back to the neighborhood-scale esthetics of earlier days.

CD2-32

The infrastructural key to this restoration plan would be the replacement of the elevated highway by a 2 kilometer tunnel built mainly beneath the south bank of the river. This would take years to build, but would eventually allow the elevated highway to be taken down, so that the strips of land now occupied by the support piers would be available as riverside green space or pedestrian promenades. The sight of the sky, the view across the river, and even the smell of fresh air, would all be restored in the long term. Projects of a similar kind have already been carried out along the Seine River in Paris, and in cities such as Düsseldorf in Germany and Seoul in South Korea.

A proposal like this was published in 2006 by a citizens group "for restoring the sky to Nihonbashi." It was backed by the prime minister of the time, Junichiro Koizumi, but then taken no further. Only the string of Coredo buildings, which will never be seen as a group until the elevated highway is gone, continues to grow as a **persistent**[8] itch to return to the idea again.

Chapter 18 A Restored View of Old Edo?

NOTES

the Muromachi section of Nihonbashi「(中央区)日本橋室町」 **Norihiko Dan** 團紀彦(1956-)日本の建築家。父は作曲家の團伊玖磨氏(1924-2001)、祖父は実業家・政治家の團伊能氏(1892-1973)、曽祖父は三井合名会社理事長の團琢磨氏(1858-1932) **the Metropolitan Expressway** 「首都高速道路」 **five great highways** 「五街道」東海道、中山道、奥州街道、日光街道、甲州街道 **the Stock Exchange** 「(東京)証券取引所」

TRUE / FALSE

Mark these statements true (T) or false (F).

1. The name Coredo is intended as a reminder of what this district was like in the Edo era.   [T / F]

2. The Metropolitan Expressway was designed to leave a clear view of both river banks.   [T / F]

3. The Metropolitan Expressway was built hurriedly for the 1964 Olympics.   [T / F]

4. The Nihonbashi district was important for various trades and businesses in the Edo era.   [T / F]

5. The overall plan of the Coredo constructions cannot be seen clearly if the Metropolitan Expressway remains as it is.   [T / F]

6. Prime Minister Koizumi opposed the idea of removing the elevated highway.   [T / F]

COMPREHENSION

Answer the questions in English.

1. What are the only places from which you can see both banks of the Nihonbashi River at once?

2. Why was the Metropolitan Expressway built overhead and along the line of the river?

3. Why is the Nihonbashi location historically significant?

4. Which financial institutions were created near the bridge in the Meiji era?

5. In what ways could the riverside and district environment be improved after the replacement of the elevated highway, according to the project supporters?

_____

GUIDED SUMMARY   CD2-33

Fill in the blanks with the words listed below.

In recent years, a series of buildings sharing the name "Coredo" have been built on both sides of the Nihonbashi River. Historically, the Nihonbashi (1_____) is a location of (2_____) importance as a road meeting point and as a commercial and financial center. But when the inner circle of the Metropolitan Expressway was built in the 1960s, one (3_____) section was constructed along the line of the Nihonbashi River, (4_____) it impossible to stand on one bank and look across at the other side. The Coredo buildings are a kind of architectural protest against this disturbance of the district's character. The only way to enjoy the whole building arrangement, and also to (5_____) the riverside views and environment of the district, would be by removing the overhead highway and (6_____) it with a tunnel.

| outstanding | elevated | making | district | restore | replacing |

COLUMN

　河川の上を通っていた高速道路を撤去して清流を復元した先例が、ソウルに見られます。日本の高度経済成長と同じように「漢江(ハンガン)の奇跡」と呼ばれた時期に、ソウルでも高速道路網が整備されました。この折に、市内を流れていた清渓川(チョンゲチョン)が地下水路と化してしまいました。2002年に高速道路撤去を公約に掲げた李明博(イ ミョンバク)氏がソウル市長に当選(その後、韓国大統領に就任)し、2005年に工事が終わりました。市民はこの動きを歓迎し、復元された清流で水に親しんでいるそうです。

　日本では、2020年の東京五輪開催決定を契機として日本橋川の上を通る高速道路撤去について議論が再燃しました。開通から半世紀を経て老朽化が進んでいることもあり、「思い切って高速道路を地下化すれば川面が取り戻せる」という意見が浮上したのです。日本橋周辺の高速道路に限らず日本の高度経済成長期に造られた社会基盤はどれもみな、更新の時期を迎えようとしています。

Cross-border Organ Transplants

CHAPTER 19

日本でも臓器移植は少しずつ増えていますが、欧州では国境を越えた移植も盛んです。ベネルクス３国とドイツ、オーストリア、スロベニア、クロアチア、ハンガリーの８カ国グループで始まった非営利組織が、協力病院を持つまでに拡大しました。北欧５国やバルト３国にも同様の仕組みがあります。米国では自動車運転免許証に臓器移植の意思表示をする制度が盛り込まれ、日本も追随しています。

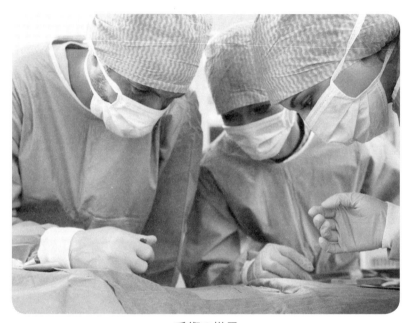

手術の様子

VOCABULARY

Match these expressions from the text with the items closest in meaning in the box below.

(1) life-support ___ (2) transplant ___ (3) irreversible ___ (4) condolence ___
(5) hereditary ___ (6) recipient ___ (7) gratitude ___ (8) consent ___

a. sympathy when someone has died	b. receiver c. feeling of thanks
d. unable to change back	e. passed down from a parent
f. equipment for keeping a patient alive	g. agreement to have something done
h. transfer of a body organ from one person to another	

READING

A family tragedy in Germany: The father dies of an aneurysm — a sudden burst in the main blood artery at the base of the brain. The moment it happens, all brain activity is cut off. He probably had no time to feel it.

He was only 50. He died totally without warning. And for a while, the rest of his body still went on functioning on **life-support**.[1] After the confirmation of brain death from two specialists, required by German law, the system was switched off. But just before that, the hospital asked his wife if she wished to allow the body organs to be donated for **transplants**.[2] She thought about it, agreed, and signed the forms. He would have wanted it. This way, part of him would still be alive and helping others to live.

Speaking more objectively about this, **irreversible**[3] brain death is the ideal condition for organ donations, because everything is left undamaged. Provided the organ tissues can be matched with those of the receivers, the chances of successful transplants are very high. Sure enough, a letter came not long afterward from the German Organ Transplant Trust. After two short sentences of **condolence**[4] and thanks, it came to the point:

After examinations and a check of the medical and legal requirements, we were able to register his heart, lungs, both kidneys and his liver with the Eurotransplant databank in Leiden, the Netherlands. Taking account of urgency and chances of success, the organs were matched with five patients and transplanted.

His heart was given to a 53-year-old man, whose own heart was so weak that only a transplant could save him. This operation went without complications, and the patient is already out of hospital.

*Both lungs went to a 51-year-old woman who had a **hereditary**[5] disease. This patient is also doing well. After many years, she is finally able to breathe properly again.*

The person who received the liver is a 37-year-old man. The organ is functioning well, so that he can look forward to a near-normal life.

The left kidney was given to a 26-year-old woman who had been on the waiting list for years and unable to live without dialysis. Now she can be released from care.

The person receiving the right kidney is a 2-year-old, with a hereditary condition that made her dependent on dialysis. The donated kidney is working so well that it is expected she will be able to go to playschool.

Even though, for legal reasons, these **recipients**[6] *will never have the chance to thank you, we know from our experience that they will always feel a special bond to their unknown donor, and a deep condolence and* **gratitude**[7] *to the donor's family.*

CD2-36

The wife found this letter touching. Of course, there are also people who disapprove of organ transplants, especially outside of the same family. They might find the letter disturbing.

"Eurotransplant" mentioned in the letter is an NGO founded in 1967 by a Dutch medical researcher called Jon van Rood. He worked with antigens, body substances which react against tissues entering from outside. Only patients with the right antigen pattern can receive a donated organ without complications. Van Rood's organization built up a database and a points system for matching donated organs with patients on transplant waiting lists. By 1970, this had grown into an international partnership. The Netherlands, Belgium, Luxemburg, Germany, Austria, Slovenia, Croatia and Hungary are now full members, with further countries interested in joining. Two other partnerships on the same model are Scandiatransplant, with Sweden, Denmark, Norway, Finland and Iceland, and Balttransplant, with Estonia, Latvia and Lithuania.

To give an idea of scale, in 2011, 2,481 organ donors were registered with Eurotransplant, providing a supply of 2,170 pairs of kidneys, 917 hearts, 1,032 pairs of lungs, 2,112 livers, and 1,008 pancreases. The take-up rate was 80 percent for kidneys and livers, 60 percent for lungs, 50 percent for hearts, and 30 percent for pancreases. In Japan that year, 112 organ donations from brain- or heart-dead people were registered, with a take-up rate of 50 percent.

Obviously, donor rates vary depending on countries and cultures. It also makes a difference whether the **consent**[8] to donate is taken by the individual before death or by the family afterward. Another factor is whether the country has an "opt-in" system, in which organs are used only with consent, or an "opt-out" system, in which they can be used unless consent is refused. In the decade of the 2000s, some U.S. states began printing on drivers' licenses whether the individual consented to donating an organ or not, and this led to a rapid increase in "yes" answers. This system is now spreading around the world, including Japan, where it is beginning to have an impact. However, European-style cross-border donor and transplant partnerships seem unlikely in Northeast Asia anytime soon.

NOTES

aneurysm「動脈瘤（りゅう）」　**complication**「合併症」　**dialysis**「透折療法」腎臓機能が低下した場合に人工的に血液を浄化する治療　**antigen**「抗原」　**pancreas**「膵臓（ずいぞう）」　**opt-in system**「"同意のみ"制」同意するという意思表示が必要　**opt-out system**「"不同意以外"制」否定の意思表示をしない限り、同意したものと見なす

TRUE / FALSE

Mark these statements true (T) or false (F).

1. In a brain death situation, brain activity continues faintly while the rest of the body is dead. [T / F]

2. It is highly likely that some of the organs donated from this patient were used in transplants outside of Germany. [T / F]

3. All of the organs were donated to the same recipient. [T / F]

4. The recipients were informed who the donor was. [T / F]

5. Eurotransplant now operates in eight central European countries and that number is likely to increase further. [T / F]

6. Organ transplants from dead patients seem to be roughly as frequent in Japan as they are in Europe. [T / F]

COMPREHENSION

Answer the questions in English.

1. For patients to receive a donated organ without complications, what condition is crucial?

   _____

2. Why are the recipients not allowed to know the identity of the dead donor?

   _____

3. What are the organ / recipient database and the points system used for?

   _____

Chapter 19 Cross-border Organ Transplants

4. Which type of organ donating system seems to suit Japan better, an opt-in or an opt-out type? Why do you think so?

   _____

5. Do you agree that cross-border donor and transplant partnerships seem unlikely in Northeast Asia? If they existed, which countries or regions might take part?

   _____

GUIDED SUMMARY CD2-37

Fill in the blanks with the words listed below.

The cross-border organ transplant partnership Eurotransplant was started in 1967 by a Dutch (1_____) in the field of antigens, substances in the body which (2_____) against the wrong patterns of transplanted tissue. To avoid giving organs to (3_____) whose bodies would reject them, the first task was to build up a (4_____) of people waiting for transplants, which also included other information such as urgency. As a result, organs available for transplant could be rapidly (5_____) with receivers' needs. Eurotransplant now covers eight countries. Other schemes for promoting organ donations are also spreading around the world. Japan has adopted an idea from the United States, in which car drivers declare on their (6_____) whether they consent to donating organs after death or not.

| database | matched | react | recipients | licenses | researcher |

COLUMN

　臓器移植の前提となる脳死については、「脳死を人の死と認めるか、否か」で論争があります。脳死に対して心臓停止は、誰が見ても「生きていない」という状態ですから、これを人の死と認めることに異論はないでしょう。しかし脳死状態の人は、平常通り心臓が動き、呼吸をしているのです。このような状態で臓器を摘出することには、宗教的・文化的な反論が出てくるのも必然と言えるのかもしれません。これは日本に限ったことではありません。欧米でも脳死による臓器移植に疑問を持つ人が見受けられます。

　脳死判定に当たっては、「不可逆的」というのが重要な基準です。これは「元に戻らない」という意味です。脳死判定では、自発呼吸ができるか確認するために一時的に人工呼吸器を外す場合もあり、患者の容体に大きな影響を及ぼす可能性があります。

The Next Two Summer Olympics: Rio and Tokyo

CHAPTER 20

夏季五輪・パラリンピックは、2016年にブラジルのリオデジャネイロで、2020年には東京で開催されることが決まっています。ブラジルで懸念されているのは、建設工事に絡む談合の存在と治安の悪さです。大都市のスラム街には行政や警察の手が及ばない地区があり、五輪などの開催に当たって対策を練ってきました。東京では、前回の五輪から半世紀以上を経て道路などの社会基盤が老朽化しています。

リオデジャネイロのコルコバードの丘に立つキリスト像

VOCABULARY

Match these expressions from the text with the items closest in meaning in the box below.

(1) entrust with ___   (2) overstrain ___   (3) legacy ___   (4) graying ___
(5) cartel ___   (6) shabby ___   (7) gentrified ___   (8) regimented ___

a. aging	b. make responsible for	c. rigidly ordered
d. past tradition	e. dirty and unattractive	f. put too great a burden on
g. a group of companies in secret agreement about price fixing		
h. once inhabited by poor people, but now upmarket		

Chapter 20   The Next Two Summer Olympics: Rio and Tokyo

READING

Hosting the Summer Olympics is an exciting but risky prospect. To be **entrusted with**[1] it, a city has to show that it is capable of putting on an inspiring but orderly program without **overstraining**[2] its finances, infrastructure or environment. Yet there is always a risk of things going wrong, turning the celebration into an embarrassment. This risk is inseparable from the opportunity of hosting the Olympics.

What opportunities and risks do the next two Olympics hold for their host cities? The 2016 Games are to be held in Rio de Janeiro in Brazil, one of the rising star "BRICS" nations which command economic power but are burdened with the **legacies**[3] of uneven progress and social inequality. The 2020 Games go to Tokyo, a **graying**[4] capital whose immediate worry is how to maintain its prosperity on a shrinking population base. Each of these cities will be moved by different expectations and fears in its preparations to add a new touch to the shared Olympic tradition.

The 2016 Games will be the first held in South America, and the impact will be all the greater coming after the 2014 soccer World Cup. The opening and closing ceremonies for both are in the Maracanã Stadium, built for the 1950 World Cup. In addition, Rio already has an Olympic Stadium, opened in 2007, which is being enlarged, and the Sambodromo, a 700-meter parade street for the Rio Carnival built in 1984. The city's problems lie more with budgeting (the Olympic Stadium cost five times its original estimate) and with construction quality (parts of the roof need replacing). There are also reports of delays with new facilities required for 2016 and with infrastructure improvements, especially sewage treatment and the subway extension for the central Olympic zone.

The biggest problems, however, concern law and order. On the one hand, since 2010, the Brazilian government has been pursuing a campaign against **cartel**[5] bidding in the construction projects. On the other, police have been trying to reduce street crime, especially targeting the favela districts in which local gangs have their strongholds.

The original "Favela" was a hill in northeastern Brazil. Soldiers who fought a rebellion there in the 1890s were resettled on a hillside in Rio which was given the same name but turned into a slum. Other hill slums followed, especially with rural immigration starting in the 1950s. This has now leveled off, and some favelas are less **shabby**.[6] But many remain under the control of mafia-like gangs. Since 2008, city authorities have been reestablishing a presence in some favelas, first by driving out open crime and then by improving services. Sometimes this seems to work, and a favela tourism, based on movie locations, takes root. But at best, only a few traders benefit. In general, as crime retreats, middle-class bargain-hunters move in, rents go up, and old residents move out in search of cheaper places in less **gentrified**[7] favelas. Some residents even protest that the authorities' real aim is to drive out the poor and let in the rich.

Compared with the more **regimented**[8] Olympics in Beijing (2008), it is difficult for the authorities in Rio to exert strong control, and in the end the solution may be for society as a whole to turn more middle-class. For now, if the problems can be kept in the background where they do not interfere with the Games, the authorities will feel relieved.

It is too early to know what message of urban renewal the 2020 Tokyo Olympics will send out to the world. But infrastructure changes will come in the form of less spectacular projects which are required anyway: transits between central Tokyo and the two airports, the restoration of the existing road system, the completion of the middle and outer expressway rings, and fuller access to the Odaiba and Ariake islands. The comments of International Olympic Committee members when the choice of Tokyo was announced in September 2013 focused on the reliability and realism of the Tokyo proposal, which is what residents appreciate too.

There were also notes of concern, however, over whether the after-effects of the Fukushima nuclear accident were really "under control" as claimed. Progress in recovery work in Tohoku will be insistently looked for as these Games draw nearer. Another risk, finally, will be the continuing coolness between Japan and its nearest neighbors, especially South Korea and China. Who is more right or wrong about past or present differences is not a question that will ever turn 2020 into a success. The key to that will be in dialog, which is a matter of trying to understand other people's hopes, fears and wishes for this world, even when you think they are wrong.

Chapter 20　The Next Two Summer Olympics: Rio and Tokyo

NOTES

BRICS ブラジル、ロシア、インド、中国、南アフリカの5カ国の頭文字を組み合わせた造語で、急速に経済力を増している「新興5カ国」を指す。　**the Maracanã stadium**「マラカナン競技場」　**bargain-hunters** 割安な住宅を求める人々　**the two airports** 羽田と成田の両空港を指す。　**Odaiba and Ariake islands**「お台場、有明」

TRUE / FALSE

Mark these statements true (T) or false (F).

1. For any city, hosting the Olympics is a burden on finances, infrastructure and environment.　[T / F]

2. Japan is now an aging society.　[T / F]

3. The 2014 soccer World Cup was the first one to be hosted in Brazil.　[T / F]

4. The origin of Rio's favela districts goes back to the end of the 18th century.　[T / F]

5. Driving out crime from the favelas and improving services seems to bring benefits to nearly all local residents.　[T / F]

6. For the coming 2020 Olympics, Tokyo will have to put more effort into new infrastructure than it did for the 1964 ones.　[T / F]

COMPREHENSION

Answer the questions in English.

1. What negative legacies are the BRICS nations still burdened with?

   _____

2. What law and order problems threaten the 2016 Rio Olympics, in business and in everyday life?

   _____

3. What negative effect can the cleaning up of the favelas have on residents' lives?

   _____

4. What sort of infrastructure developments are wanted for the 2020 Tokyo Olympics, compared with the ones needed for 1964?

   _____

5. Do you generally agree with the claim that the Fukushima nuclear accident is under control so far as the 2020 Olympics are concerned? Why or why not?

___

GUIDED SUMMARY

Fill in the blanks with the words listed below.

Hosting the Summer Olympics is a (1 _____) venture for any city. A lot has to be spent on developing urban (2 _____) such as highways and transportation systems, and while some of the event (3 _____) may go on being used in the future, others bring no lasting (4 _____). Compared with Rio, Tokyo should have fewer problems with its second hosting of the Olympics in 2020. The proposal the city presented was marked by (5 _____) and realism. But risks remain from the possible (6 _____) of the 2011 Fukushima accident and from continuing unfriendly relations among neighboring countries in the region.

| facilities | benefits | reliability | risky | infrastructure | after-effects |

COLUMN

　「ブラジル政府が治安に不安を持つのも当然」という経験——以下は著者の1人が2007年に実際に体験した事実です。リオデジャネイロ中心部、コルコバードの丘に向かう市電カリオカ線始発停留所の近くで、人通りの少ない日曜の昼下がりでした。カメラを首からぶら下げて——本体はバッグの中に入れていたものの、首にかけたひもは見えていました——歩いていると、前から来た若い男2人が、カメラに手をかけて持ち去ろうとしました。大声を上げて抵抗すると何も取らずに立ち去りましたが、怖い経験でした。「日曜の昼間、街のど真ん中」というと日本では物騒ではない状況ですが、欧米では日曜はお店が休みで人通りが少ないことがあります。治安状況が改善されないことには、サッカーのワールドカップと同様に、これからの五輪開催にも不安を感じます。

Follow-up Reading

For readers who want to explore the 20 topic areas in this book further, here is a list of just two information sources per topic, chosen to be accessible and to give a broad or vivid picture. For instructors, many of these contain parts that could be adapted into additional class materials. Sources directly consulted in the making of this book are marked with a star (*).

Chapter 1: Shinagawa-Nagoya in 40 Minutes, 40 Meters beneath the Ground
nippon.com (Nov. 5, 2013) "Does Japan Need a High-speed Maglev Line?"
  http://www.nippon.com/en/features/h00041/ (also in Japanese)
㈱東海旅客鉄道（2013年9月）「（東京都―名古屋市間）環境影響評価準備書のあらまし」*
  http://company.jr-central.co.jp/company/others/prestatement/_pdf/alloutline.pdf

Chapter 2: AKB and the Music Promotion World
秋元康、田原総一郎（2013年）「AKB48の戦略！秋元康の仕事術」、株式会社アスコム*
Martin, Ian, *nippon.com* (Aug. 8, 2014) "AKB48: The return of Idol Music and the Rise of the Superfan" (also in Japanese)
  http://www.nippon.com/en/column/g00207

Chapter 3: Mount Fuji: The Responsibilities of Heritage
UNESCO World Heritage Center (2013) "Fujisan, sacred place and source of artistic inspiration," World Heritage List, Ref. 1418*
  http://whc.unesco.org/en/list/1418
nikkei4946.com（2013年1月1日）「富士山が世界遺産～世界遺産登録のメリットと課題を知る」
  https://www.nikkei4946.com/zenzukai/detail.aspx?zenzukai=115

Chapter 4: Tasty Vegetables: How much Extra would you Pay for them?
Soil Association (Mar., 2014) *Soil Association Organic Market Report 2014 (Report 2013*)
  http://www.soilassociation.org/marketreport
Blackmore, Nicole, *The Telegraph* (Aug. 26, 2013) "Are organic veg boxes worth the money?" * http://www.telegraph.co.uk/finance/personalfinance/consumertips/household-bills/10260573/Are-organic-veg-boxes-worth-the-money.html

Chapter 5: Can Cars Drive themselves? And who is to Blame when they Crash?
English, Andrew, *The Telegraph* (Jan. 16, 2014) "Autonomous cars – is this the end of driving?"*
  http://www.telegraph.co.uk/motoring/road-safety/10570935/Autonomous-cars-is-this-the-end-of-driving.html
Lewis, Truman, *Consumer Affairs* (Jan. 6, 2014) "RAND study: Benefits of self-driving cars outweigh the drawbacks"*
  http://www.consumeraffairs.com/news/rand-study-benefits-of-self-driving-cars-outweigh-the-drawbacks-010614.html

Chapter 6: Germany's Departure from Nuclear Energy
Smedley, Tim, *The Guardian* (May 10, 2013) "Goodbye nuclear power: Germany's renewable energy revolution"*
  http://www.theguardian.com/sustainable-business/nuclear-power-germany-renewable-energy
宇津宮尚子、*Huffington Post*（2013年11月1日）「脱原発『エネルギーシフト実現は"戦い"』ドイツのエネルギー政策シュタンツェル駐日大使に聞く」*
  http://www.huffingtonpost.jp/2013/10/31/volker-stanzel-interview-energy-shift_n_4186441.html

Chapter 7: Lest the World Forget: History as Storytelling
東京新聞（2013年8月18日）「語り部」世界と日本大図解シリーズ No. 1108*
　　http://www.tokyo-np.co.jp/article/daizukai/2013/CK2013081602100011.html
Hersey, John (1946) *Hiroshima*, New York: Alfred A. Knopf; London: Penguin Books

Chapter 8: Eel and Tuna: Tastes the Next Generation may never Know?
一般社団法人マリのフォーラム21，（2014年）「マグロ養殖の現状」*
　　http://www.yousyokugyojyou.net/index4.htm
Kanda Akemi, Katori Keisuke, Narusawa Dai, Kodera Yoichiro, *The Asahi Shimbun* (Jun. 13, 2014) "Japanese eels listed as endangered species; restaurants fear the worst"
　　http://ajw.asahi.com/article/behind_news/social_affairs/AJ201406130043

Chapter 9: Still Applying to Join the Euro
Europa Portal (Jul. 19, 2011) "Towards a single currency: a brief history of EMU"*
　　http://europa.eu/legislation_summaries/economic_and_monetary_affairs/introducing_euro_practical_aspects/125007_en.htm
原田和義、*europe magazine*（2014年1月15日）「ラトビアが18番目のユーロ導入国に」
　　http://www.eumag.jp/behind/d0114

Chapter 10: Female Athletes Dramatized
矢内由美子、*nippon.com*（2014年2月24日）「世界のファンを魅了した浅田真央のジャンプ」* (also in English)
　　http://www.nippon.com/ja/column/g00155
Yamamoto Nasuka, *The Asahi Shimbun* (Aug. 10, 2012) "Gold Medalist/ Yoshida's dad always in her corner"*
　　http://ajw.asahi.com/article/behind_news/sports/AJ201208100050

Chapter 11: Islands of Safety – or Baby Hatches?
Xinhua Net (Mar. 17, 2014) "Suspension of baby hatch highlights abandoned infants dilemma"*
　　http://news.xinhuanet.com/english/indepth/2014-03/17/c_133193247.htm
蓮田太二（2014年1月20日）「『赤ちゃんポスト』ができるまで〜慈恵病院・蓮田病院長が語る」*
　　http://blogos.com/article/78275

Chapter 12: Pirating and Streaming: Paying our Share for Media Entertainment
Savage, Maddy, *BBC News* (Apr. 15, 2013) "Digital music: Can streaming save music sales?"*
　　http://www.bbc.com/news/business-22064353
Saison, Kelsie, PipelineProject (Jul. 23, 2012) "The Open Music Model Predicts the Future"*
　　http://pipelineproject.org/news/the-openmusic-model-predicts-the-future

Chapter 13: Print-out Pistols: How Far should Freedoms Go?
産経ニュース，（2014年5月9日）「３Ｄプリンターは諸刃の剣　『産業革命』も多様化する悪用　法則規制求める声も」*
　　http://sankei.jp.msn.com/affairs/news/140509/crm14050919540014-n1.htm
Campbell-Dollaghan, Kelsie, on *Gizmodo* (Dec. 3, 2013) "How 3D Printers Are Cranking Out Eyes, Bones, and Blood Vessels"
　　http://gizmodo.com/how-doctors-are-printing-bones-eyes-noses-and-blood-1474983505

Chapter 14: Smart Reality: Computer Games Return to the Physical World
Connellan, Nick, *broadsheet.com* (Apr. 29, 2014) *"Entering the Escape Room"*
 http://www.broadsheet.com.au/melbourne/art-and-design/article/entering-escape-room
Giant Bomb (2008) *Maniac Mansion**
 http://giantbomb.com/maniac-mansion/3030-2037

Chapter 15: Seven Days, Six Nights and a Run: A Special Interest Tour
New York Road Runners (2014) *TCS New York City Marathon 11.02.14* *
 http://www.tcsnycmarathon.org
株式会社DOGエアーサービス（2014年）「ニューヨークシティマラソンツアー2014」*
 http://www.marathon-tour.com/tour/index.html

Chapter 16: Fracking: Cracks in the Ground beneath our Feet
Anderson, Richard, *BBC News* (Apr. 6, 2014) "Shale industry faces global reality check"
 http://www.bbc.com/news/business-26735000
nikkei4946.com（2014年3月3日）「『シェール革命』で何が変わる？日本への影響は？」*
 https://www.nikkei4946.com.zenzukai/detail.aspx?/zenzukai=130

Chapter 17: Two World Heritage Food Traditions: Washoku and Kimchi
Kumakura, Isao (Jan. 30, 2014) Interview: "*Washoku*, traditional dietary cultures of the Japanese" in *Discuss Japan: Japan Foreign Policy Forum**
 http://www.japanpolicyforum.jp/en/archives/culture/pt20140130140607.html
UNESCO Culture Sector (2013) "Kimjang: making and sharing kimchi in the Republic of Korea," Representative List of Intangible Cultural Heritage, Inscription 00881*
 http://www.unesco.org/culture/ich/RL/00881

Chapter 18: A Restored View of Old Edo?
株式会社三井不動産 (2014) 「『日本橋再生計画』日本橋のあゆみ」
 http://www.nihonbashi-tokyo.jp/revitalization
日本橋川に空を取り戻す会 （2006年9月）「日本橋地域から始まる新たな街づくりにむけて（提言）」*
 http://www.nihonbashi-michikaigi.jp/pdf/teigen02.pdf

Chapter 19: Cross-border Organ Transplants?
畑川剛毅 （2010年3月22日）「医療機器の最先端治療の現場を歩く：[第一回]新型の人工心臓を次々に臨床現場へ―ドイツの心臓病センター」、朝日新聞グローブ*
 http://globe.asahi.com/feature/100322/side/02_01.html
Eurotransplant International Foundation (as of 2014) "About Eurotransplant"*
 http://www.eurotransplant.org/cms/index.php?page=about_brief

Chapter 20: The Next Two Summer Olympics: Rio and Tokyo
Olympic.org (Mar. 21, 2014) "IOC tells Rio 2016 that there is not a moment to lose"*
 http://www.olympic.org/news/ioc-tells-rio-2016-that-there-is-not-a-moment-to-lose/227767
毎日新聞（2014年6月28日）「東京：五輪見据え開発も加速　一味違う『らしさ』演出へ」
 http://mainichi.jp/sports/news/20140628k0000e040213000c.html

TEXT PRODUCTION STAFF

edited by	編集
Eiichi Kanno	菅野 英一
Kimio Sato	佐藤 公雄

English-language editing by	英文校閲
Bill Benfield	ビル・ベンフィールド

cover design by	表紙デザイン
Ruben Frosali	ルーベン・フロサリ

text design by	本文デザイン
Ruben Frosali	ルーベン・フロサリ

CD PRODUCTION STAFF

narrated by	吹き込み者
Rachel Walzer (AmE)	レイチェル・ウォルツァー (アメリカ英語)
Bill Sullivan (AmE)	ビル・サリバン (アメリカ英語)

本書にはCD（別売）があります。
2枚組　5,000円（税別）

Searching the Future, Reviewing the Past
世界を語る、日本を語る

2015年1月20日　初版発行
2015年1月31日　第2刷発行

著　者　David Dykes
　　　　角岡　賢一

発行者　佐野　英一郎

発行所　株式会社 成 美 堂
　　　　〒101-0052　東京都千代田区神田小川町3-22
　　　　TEL 03-3291-2261　FAX 03-3293-5490
　　　　https://www.seibido.co.jp

印　刷　倉敷印刷(株)
製　本　(有)秀美堂製本所

ISBN 978-4-7919-3393-8　　　　　　　　　　　　　　Printed in Japan

・落丁・乱丁本はお取り替えします。
・本書の無断複写は、著作権上の例外を除き著作権侵害となります。